SUICIDE
DICTIONARY

Paul Lonely

First published by O Books, 2007
O Books is an imprint of John Hunt Publishing Ltd.,
The Bothy, Deershot Lodge, Park Lane, Ropley, Hants, SO24 0BE, UK
office1@o-books.net
www.o-books.net

Distribution in:

UK and Europe
Orca Book Services
orders@orcabookservices.co.uk
Tel: 01202 665432 Fax: 01202 666219 Int. code (44)

USA and Canada
NBN
custserv@nbnbooks.com
Tel: 1 800 462 6420 Fax: 1 800 338 4550

Australia and New Zealand
Brumby Books
sales@brumbybooks.com.au
Tel: 61 3 9761 5535 Fax: 61 3 9761 7095

Far East (offices in Singapore, Thailand, Hong Kong, Taiwan)
Pansing Distribution Pte Ltd
kemal@pansing.com
Tel: 65 6319 9939 Fax: 65 6462 5761

South Africa
Alternative Books
altbook@peterhyde.co.za
Tel: 021 447 5300 Fax: 021 447 1430

Text copyright Paul Lonely 2007

Design: Stuart Davies

ISBN: 978 1 84694 061 3

A CIP catalogue record for this book is available from the British Library.

Printed in the US by Maple Vail

SUICIDE
DICTIONARY

The History of
RAINBOW ABBEY

Paul Lonely

BOOKS

Winchester, UK
Washington, USA

CONTENTS

Genius. Paul Lonely has gifted the world with a genuinely unique work. Suicide Dictionary is a miraculous kaleidoscope of perspectives bound to stretch the mind, body and spirit of its lucky readership.
Stuart Davis, author of *Love Has No Opposite*

An ambitious project, brilliantly executed, exhibiting the integral thinking so vital to our present age.
Ron Miller, Religion Department, Lake Forest College, author of *The Gospel of Thomas: A Guidebook for Spiritual Practice.*

Beautiful and provocative. Suicide Dictionary is a masterful poetic synthesis of western cognition and eastern spirituality.
Malena Gamboa, One Mind Village

One of the most promising young writers we've ever encountered.
Integral Spiritual Center

What an epic! Poetry, intellect and humor combine to invoke a deeply resonant spirituality that awakens the reader on multiple levels.
Dr Lin Morel, author of *Peace at the Center*

The first trans-traditional scripture written from a fully awakened integral awareness.
Dustin DiPerna, author of *The Infinite Ladder: An Introduction to Integral Religious Studies.*

*A "Suicide Dictionary" by a man named Lonely? What's going on here?
In my opinion, it's a new genre of literature: an integral interweaving of
the pre-modern wisdom of the past with the post-modern insights of the
present, a skilful and intriguing inquiry into not only a lexicon of words
but the essence of all the world's religions interspersed with modern
characters trying to make sense of it all. Let the words and ideas on these
pages connect your synapses in ways that you never perceived of before
while reading this integral text of sparkling gems meant for contem-
plation. It will make you want to live again-but this time, integrally!*
Brad Reynolds, author of *Embracing Reality: The Integral Vision of Ken
Wilber*

*Ken Wilber is apparently fond of telling Paul that his readers haven't
been born yet. (Henry Miller says loneliness is a prerequisite for great art
- how appropriate.) I have to disagree with Ken – breathlessly, having to
stop in awe after nearly every passage, I read "Suicide Dictionary", and I
loved it.*
Michael Garfield

*This is a startlingly original work of sheer genius – highly recommended,
if you can handle it.*
Ken Wilber, author of *The Integral Vision*

FOREWORD

BY DUSTIN DIPERNA

Far too often, books represent a mediocre reflection of all that's come before; the same ideas expressed in different words – identical textures softly dissected and examined by the intellect of fresh readers. Creativity exists to be sure…but for the most part, works of art and writing remain lost in a sea of normalcy. Creativity drifts into the trap of our culturally conditioned expectations; budding ideas are restricted to the dominant center of gravity of our collective level of consciousness. As if translating a sentence from one language to another, artistic expressions are often nothing more than creative translations. The alterations are superficial, horizontal in nature. The depth and meaning behind the expressions remain unchanged. Thus stands 99% of all that we read, see, and enjoy. We are left today with a boiling pot of *horizontal* creativity.

As literary and artistic consumers, we are seldom offered novel gifts expressed from an entirely new level of awareness. Rarely are we exposed to ideas that have thrashed free from our cultural molds in order to honor a place of genuine authenticity. Every once in a while, however, there is a break in the pattern and a work of literature emerges that is truly unique. Sometimes a book presents itself that is so novel, it actually transcends the boundaries of the norm. On these rare occasions, we bear witness to a vertical shift in literary dimension. New levels of depth and meaning are manifested instantaneously. When these unique flowers blossom we, as readers, are offered an opportunity to ride the sweet scent of *vertical* creativity. When pieces of literary genius are able to break the mold of normalcy and preconditioned patterns they provide us all with a chance to evolve consciousness to the next inevitable stage. Transcending but including all that has come before it, the fruits of *vertical* creativity are transformative.

Paul Lonely's *Suicide Dictionary* is a perfect example of transformative literature. Representing a vertical shift of literary potential, *Suicide Dictionary* is saturated with exuberance and novelty. Finding new ways to transmit both ancient and modern dharma alike, *Suicide Dictionary* introduces us to both a new form of authorship as well as an entirely fresh experience as a reader. *Suicide Dictionary* is vertical creativity at its best.

Suicide Dictionary asks the reader to let go and to trust the unfolding of the story. Smashing through all convention, the story of the monks at Rainbow Abbey sweeps the reader away as if floating on a raft down a stream. The standard life vest the reader is so accustomed to, such as character introduction, chronological sequence of time, even plot and climax, are thrown over board. The reader is instead invited to trust — trust the story, trust the process, and most of all to trust the author. Written from the unique altitude of an integral awareness, Paul Lonely's work offers us one of the first examples of integral literature.

To conclude, it is important to notice that throughout *Suicide Dictionary* Paul Lonely is not merely *tolerating* all of our beautiful religious traditions. It is also of the essence to note that neither is he engaging in a post-modern nonchalant relativistic dance. Although both of these positions are to be highly commended, the reader is invited to discover that Paul Lonely is approaching his work from a compassionate integral awareness and is thus able to *fully and authentically embrace* all traditions *at once*. This capacity to authentically embrace all traditions simultaneously may very well be the beginning of a new tradition in and of itself. One that is ready (and may be calling for) it's own set of wisdom books.

In years to come, *Suicide Dictionary* will be looked upon as a work of art regardless of what level of consciousness the reader might bring to its pages. Its flowing stanzas leave silk strands of wisdom for those at rational, pluralistic, and mythic levels alike. But for those lucky few souls who can meet each word, each reflection, and each poem with an integral lens, *Suicide Dictionary* sings back in perfect harmony. The resonance that emerges when the altitudes of reader and author meet on equal ground is nothing less than divine. As turquoise notes drift away in the wind, the reader is left riding a chord of bliss.

Overflowing,
Dustin DiPerna
New York, Spring 2007

www.infiniteladder.com

NOTES FROM THE AUTHOR

I.

This book is the first volume of what I intend to be a life-long work. It is both literary and spiritual in nature. Like Whitman's *Leaves of Grass*, *Suicide Dictionary* will advance piecemeal as I continue with my goal of offering a "Contemporary Upanishads" that captures the beauty of both western intellectuality and eastern (or mystical) spirituality in a single literary framework. The closeness of my integral vision with the work of Ken Wilber will be obvious to the initiated. I have applied Mr. Wilber's Integral Theory to the making of *Suicide Dictionary* and now consider it's poetic expression an announcement of the emergence of an Integral Poetics, a sub-section of Integral Art. Although I am as yet employing poetic *forms* of the past, the ideas erupting from the symbols I offer are products of consciously operating from (at least) an "integral" or "second tier" level of awareness.

This volume of *Suicide Dictionary* consists of the first 100 entries. The headers are taken from the 'A' section of my Merriam Webster's Collegiate Dictionary. The book is and will continue to be divided into chapters of 50 entries each.

Each entry's purpose is four-fold:

1) To supply a "*definition*" for the corresponding word.
2) To supply a snippet of "integral philosophy" through the use of poetic language.
3) To supply a trans-rational pointing exercise that encourages the reader to explore spiritual experience through an *authentic* transformative practice of their choice.
4) To supply information which develops the main story-line in regards to the epic of *Quantum Psalter* and Rainbow Abbey.

I plan to use this existence to define each word in the 'A' section of the dictionary. This leaves the opportunity for other integral writers to take action on B, C, D, etc… A project such as this has the potential of offering a truly "Worldcentric Vedas" to the emerging Integral Age. If you are interested in authoring a future volume of Suicide Dictionary please contact me via my website at www.suicidedictionary.com

When I was an undergraduate science major at a small college in central Kentucky there was a poster hanging in one of my classrooms which read, "What *isn't* Chemistry?". I remember instantly identifying the reductionistic nature of the phrase and thinking at the time, "What *isn't* Mind?". It's now been six years since I sat in that classroom. The road I've taken is embedded in each word of this book. As I sit here today staring into the depths of what IS, I can only hope that one day this phrase will be added to that poster: "What *isn't* Spirituality?".

II.

It has recently been brought to my attention that a short summary to properly situate the reader would be beneficial before beginning the book. Although I feel the note above will be sufficient for most readers, I've decided to provide a bit of background information that will allow the reader to grasp from the out-set some of the more surface aspects of the work.

The setting for *Suicide Dictionary* is a monastery named Rainbow Abbey which is located on an island in the North Atlantic called Ambrojjio. This island was discovered in 1453 ce and donated, later in the same year, to the Catholic Church. Pope Nicholas V (the first humanist Pope) used the land to erect a secret monastery for an artist colony of monk-poets he employed to formulate what he called a "prophetic" or "inspired" document to be published in the year 2050 . This artist colony (now called the Order of Quantum Catholics) has survived to the present day (2007) and still employs monk-poets who remain hard at work on Pope Nicholas's "prophetic" document which has now been titled *Quantum Psalter*.

There are nine monk-poets currently living at Rainbow Abbey and working on *Quantum Psalter*. Their names are:

Taft Merryweather

Abbot Ezra Davenport

Silas Paul

Gordon Flannery

Dale Rutherford

Issak Kidwell

Abe Hendrik

Martin Fugat

Simon Warner

There is also a young boy, named Hugo Gustafson, who figures prominently in the book. His mother is an oblate at Rainbow Abbey and allows Hugo (a prized student) to spend some of his free time with the Quantums.

Thus far I have utilized multiple *styles* in my presentation of Suicide Dictionary. Each entry's style will fall into one of four categories:

1) *Dialogues*. The majority of entries are composed of conversations between Quantum monk-poets currently residing at Rainbow Abbey.

2) *Direct prose statements*. These entries have one of two purposes. The first is to give details of the physical features of Rainbow Abbey (an example is entry #3). The other is to provide a brief history of the Order of Quantum Catholics (examples are entries #20 and 27).

3) *Free-standing poems*. In Book One I have written a series of sonnets. In Book Two I have included six acrostics.

4) *Journal Entries*. These entries furnish Quantum history and insights from the monk-poets of Rainbow Abbey's past.

As you begin the book please do not be put off by not having a feel for "who the characters are." It is my intention to transcend and include this "cult of personality." As my dictionary progresses I will slowly fill in the character's *masks* for those interested. What the monks are saying and *pointing to* is far more important. That being said, the characters will mean more and more to you as the book advances. Nirvana will hold hands with Samsara, I promise.

Paul Lonely
Autumn 2006

In 1453, Muslim poet and navigator, Ahmad ibn Majid, crashed into the
shores of an unknown island
Enfolded in the following pages is a history of the artist colony turned
monastery that bloomed from our navigators unexpected find.

This is the heart-beat of Rainbow Abbey.

BOOK ONE

SHAKESPEARE'S HAZING

1 [1]A IS FOR AXIAL

Tasmanianly swiveling in his swiveling chair, freshly inaugurated into monkdom pledging life-long vows in a commitment to the Quantums at Rainbow Abbey, Taft Merryweather, part-time Buddhist, neo-Sufi sympathizer, amateur botanist, collegiate athlete, Rhodes Scholar, and literary tycoon from Regent's Park College (Oxford); plus aspiring reformer of trans-Benedictine monastic law, stops dizzy and stares at the brown-robed vibrations buzzing in the corridor.

——Congratulations Were-wolf, Silas Paul says constructing a cross in plain view through Merryweather's door with his index fingers.

——And may peace be upon you, Abe Hendrik says. Father, father, and father spirit, amen.

The speckles that are Silas Paul and Abe Hendrik gradually settle into focus.

——Allahu akbar, Sri Krishna, cookies and milk, Merryweather replies exposing a playful gap-toothed smile through a thicket of red-black beard.

——*Lectio Divina*, Taft, t minus seven minutes and counting! Silas Paul says. *Muid ad-Din ibn al-Arabi* with a pinch of *Rumi* and *Shariah* for me. What about you?

Whirling dervishes in America. Shock value.

——*The Scarlet Letter*, I guess, Merryweather says.

[2]A

Tangible angels we are One and All,
Under and over and inside the flesh;—
There is no frontier for World-centric to draw,

If truly world-centric the angel has meshed.

A Stupa was built on the sands of Iran,

Each native said prayers and accepted its worth;

They all remained Muslim and nothing was gone,

But added to Islam was Buddhism's birth.

Allah as a Baby was from Jewish men,

Which leaked to Muhammad who Journeyed at Night;

The Prophet was tested but mastered zazen,

And now simply twirls as a Dervish in white.

    A relic of Buddha in Mecca will stand,

       When Islamic integrals…

                open this Land.

2 ¹AAH IS FOR ISLAM, OO IS FOR HINDU

After dawn *Salat* and Thursday morning Mass, Taft Merryweather and Martin Fugat opt for an early breakfast. They fumble, in a sleepy-headed daze, through a pasture fuzzed even further by a sugary appetizer of pixie sticks and dum-dums. The red stones they are following lead them to a gate that reads: *The Circle of Gardens, c.e. 1978.* Entering, they wind the familiar maze of shaggy box-woods and crunchy shells, eventually navigating to a black wooden sign hammered between an oval of highbush cranberry and sun-flower. In multiple languages, fluorescent orange letters and pictograms stack into a totem pole of faces grinning with the same message: *Organization of Organized Star-Dust→Rainbow Abbey's Wild Edibles!*

——Pop quiz! Martin Fugat says lifting a porcelain bowl from the cupped hands of Silas Pauls' marble representation of the Hindu goddess, *Saraswati*.

A collection of rain-water and leaf-bits are flung from the bowl.

——Where's *Krishna*? Merryweather asks dodging the liquid portion of Martin's projectile.

——Silas, Martin Fugat says, had him carried to Gordon at the planetarium. Something about the sun and moon were before the vegetation.

Taft observes Martin's periwinkle fingers. Clean nails. Accurate, conservative plucking.

——Fruit, Martin says, from the fairy bells. Sour and bitter combo from the fireweed shoots. Fennel seeds, licorice roots, and pennycress leaves. For dessert, raspberries and pixie sticks.

——Beautiful, Merryweather says. Fruit from the *disporum trachycapum*. Sour and bitter from the *epilobium angustifolium*. Fennel, I forget. *Glycyrriza lepidota* and *thlaspi arvense*. For dessert, *rubus idaeus* and *baton of sucre*.

——Almost, Martin says chewing a mouthful of salad. B-minus and a chance for redemption. *If Saladin had four arms in a Polaroid, what would he hold in the palm of each hand?*

Thinking.

——Strawberry pie. French tickler. Taj Mahal. Mushroom cloud, Merryweather says.

——Now A-plus, Martin Fugat says.

²AAH IS FOR ISLAM, OO IS FOR HEBREW

Two Quantum Catholics critique the Crusades, the Balfour Declaration, and the optimistic future of Rainbow Abbey.

——*Single Vision* is viewing the problem from one perspective only, Abe Hendrik says. So *Double Vision* is the advancement to two.

——Problem is, Taft Merryweather says, there are three parties involved in this conflict.

——Which makes *Triple Vision* the primary goal, Abe Hendrik says.

——Ideally, Taft Merryweather says in agreement. We prefer Christians, Jews, and Muslims *together*.

³AAH

The coal in your hand is sketching on paper,
Your muscles are moving connected to Mind;
You feel you are made but also the Maker,
The Portrait you're drawing to nothing will bind.
Silhouettes of this face cascade on your Wall,
The contours are rounded, erotic, and pure;
But when this Wall crumbles post-partum your Fall,
The Stillness that's missing is Krishna's allure.
I speak as an Artist involved with your death,
Your dieing is dead to my death at your door;
This Secret begins when you're counting your breath,
And find that the Ground is the sound of your Roar.
　　These Lions and Tigers inside of your zoo,
　　Will die to themselves…
　　　　　　　　　　but revamp into You.

3 ¹AARDVARK AND AARDWOLF

Red stepping stones lead to *The Circle of Gardens*, blue to *The Field of Sculptures*, and yellow to *The Hall of Vertebrates* (complete with giraffes, elephants, cat-houses, reptile stations, equine stables, aquariums, and aviaries).

²AARDVARK AND AARDWOLF

I laugh at this body, Impermanence near,
It's more like a Bubble than Statue in might;
Still I'm in awe that my figure is Here,
I cherish it now as a Basis for Light.
Engaging two eyes, three Jewels may appear,

If Buddha and Sangha and Dharma you trust;
Or maybe I cry showing God is a Tier,
Which triggers all Buddhas to freely combust.
The stroke down my cheek is the glaze from a snail,
It glistens from laughter and sadness alive;
But Fire is the Ground and it burns without fail,
Before and then after my carcass has died.

 Wholesome are deeds in respect to the norm,

 Form is my Empty…

   and Empty my Form.

4 ¹AARON(IC)

——High priest of the Hebrews and Muslim prophet, Issak Kidwell says. Once made his walking stick into a python.

——I feel drunk, Simon Warner says. Happy, sad, and crazy at the same time.

——Happens, doesn't it, Issak Kidwell says. But there's more. He played hard-ball politics with Pharaoh in place of his stuttering brother, Moses. He cloned frogs and buried Egypt knee-deep in gnats. Even turned rivers to blood, rods to almonds, and tormented his enemies with boils from ashes that missed God's autoclave.

——Drunker, sadder, crazier, Simon Warner says massaging his temples.

Over-head, the intercom pops, squeaks, and whines.

——Don't forget Melchizedek, Abbot Ezra squawks through the speaker.

Taft saunters by, shoeless. A copy of *The Tao of Physics* and Abbot Ezra's novel, *Sibling Rivalries*, cuffed in his hand.

——Grab the Vulgate and the Seventy, Issak Kidwell says.

——Always *Triple Vision*, Simon Warner says.

[2]AARON

Ethereal Habits and History's Growth,
Are flying in sync to interpret the True;
Enlightened are Angels when products of Both
Are able to humble the Mind they imbue.
Non-local are neighbors when this Scene appears,
A New Land of Depth is now processing Light;
Locating new Space is like switching careers
From managing Darkness to owning the Bright.
When arrows of quadrants are ready to fly,
The eye of My archer is aimed at your Heart;
The True with its Goodness and Beauty comply,
Announcing This Wholeness that's also a Part.
    The tip of this dart is now surfing the air,
    With casualties preaching…
                    its infinite care.

5 [1]NORMAL AB-NORMAL

Mid-night at the dining hall. Dale Rutherford and Gordon Flannery under plumes of undulating candle-light.

——Just translate it, Gordon Flannery pleads, invisible tears pooling in his eyes. Translate *Ehyeh-Asher-Ehyeh*.

Dale Rutherford rustles the pages of his *Tanakh*, adjusts his glasses, and reads.

——I am who I am, Dale Rutherford says. Or on second thought, *I am what I shall be*.

——Hold it! Gordon Flannery pipes. If you would, repeat the second.

——*I am what I shall be*, Dale Rutherford says with a cautious blink.

In short blue under-pants, white cotton t-shirt, muscular thighs, and heavy beard; Taft Merryweather enters through a set of sturdy double doors, medieval in appearance, scavenging coffee. He curtsies for Gordon and Dale, pretending to pinch the frills of his cock-tail dress.

——Frogs and crickets are competing to out-scream one another, Merryweather says pirouetting into the kitchen and away from the conversation.

——Elohim, you see, Gordon Flannery says to Rutherford, had no history of his own. A closer reading can suggest that he didn't even know who he was.

——So they believe Elohim-Yahweh has evolved and is evolving, Dale Rutherford says.

——Yes, Gordon Flannery says. With us and with everything around us.

——Trial and error, Dale Rutherford says.

——Precisely, Gordon Flannery says. Like a child.

²AB

My halo was made in a Mystical Bower,
By Integral Angels with paraffin Souls;
This nimbus I wore to a Protestant Tower,
And deepened the Angels of Protestant goals.
I spoke from the alter of Trinity's grace,
In parables after the Gospel was read;
I spoke of their God-head as Primeval Face,
While adding this scripture that Jesus had said:
All torsos are lanterns with candles inside,
Their wicks are the spines where the chakras have bloomed;
Our energy jumps when these lanterns collide,
But wax from these candles is never consumed.
    Endless are embers arriving from Ground,
      Igniting this Neon…
                  to which We are bound.

6 ¹SIMON WARNER'S ABA

In the direction of the sun, airplanes and helicopters whiz through dumplings of crinoline clouds. Abe Hendrik, watching Simon Warner from a bench in the shade, warmly absorbs the waves of sound and light and swims in the fizz it leaves in his heels. A crescent at each peak.

——Let's fly, Abe Hendrik says. And be in love. And drink tea. And write suras and psalters until our minds go dry.

——Sounds wonderful, Simon Warner says sprinkling acorns on the grass. But first let's whisper a prayer to Saint Francis and feed *zakat* to the animals.

Both close their eyes and tilt their heads chin to breast.

——And he is beautiful, Simon Warner says, and jocund and robust and strong. We praise *with* thou, Yahweh-Elohim, and our sister Mother Earth, who sustains and governs us, and produces various fruits with colored flowers and herbage. Praise and bless with Allah, we give our thanks and receive them back with great humility. Amen.

——Amen, Abe Hendrik says peeping into the pockets of Simon Warner's shirt.

A vial of cherry-red sugar water for the humming-birds. Fractions of wheat and pumpernickel for the cardinals and robins. Carrots and peppermints for the miniature ponies. A cantaloupe rind for the goat.

——And for the two little monkeys blessed with the gift of third-tier consciousness? Abe Hendrik asks.

——Check the other pocket, Simon Warner says.

——The Recitation and King James, Abe Hendrik says.

——With lemonade and clean sheets of paper in the library, Simon Warner says.

——*Zakat*! Abe Hendrik shouts. And double scoops of vanilla ice-cream topped with a sprig of mint.

²ABA

When staircases swirl with no objects in sight,
You tinker with physics and thoughts of the moon;
When dolphins are jumping enhancing the Light,
You giggle at mid-night and laugh until noon.
When captors of Spirit are peddling their Chain,
You open so wide they can't measure your girth;
When science is picking philosophy's brain,
You chuckle in silence at thoughts of your birth.
This joke you've discovered is kosmically free,
The sound of its koan is comically True;
Your one hand is clapping while twisting the key
To locks of your laughter and mystical view.
　　Old Patterns of Habit will deeply improve,
　　As Clowns of your polis…
　　　　　　　　are carving their Groove.

7 ¹ABACA

——The banana, Taft Merryweather says to a crowded lecture hall, is any variety of tropical or sub-tropical plants of the genus *Musa* that bear clusters of long yellow or reddish fruits. There are sixty-seven species and more than two hundred varieties of *Musa*. Bananas may have been cultivated as early as one thousand years before the birth of *Yeshua* in the rain forests of Southeast Asia, and are mentioned in the Buddhist Pali manuscripts dating back to the sixth century bce. *Arabs brought the fruit to the Middle East and Africa in the seventh century.* In 1482 the Portuguese found bananas growing as a staple food on Africa's west coast in what are now Gambia, Sierra Leone, and Liberia, and transplanted them to the Canary Islands. From here, the Franciscan monk, Tomas de Berlanga, brought rootstocks to the Caribbean island of Santo Domingo in the year

1516 of the common era.

²ABACA

In this fraction of fire on an island of sand,
The bush is still burning that Yahweh inspired;
Removing his sandals and touching this land,
A rabbi with Moses to Temple retired.
A bishop was there when the rabbi returned,
The sand was still holy but pressed into glass;
The bush was still flaming where Yahweh had burned,
But now his New Name was exalted at Mass.
On two diff'rent Mondays the Christian and Jew,
Inspected a Mosque that was built on their ground;
Six hundred years since they first traded views,
These Muslims were fanning the bush Moses found.
   Translations are seen by my widening Gyre,
   Enabling reaction…
                  to Sermons of Fire.

8 ¹ABACK

Three shiny yellow ponchos playing in the rain.

——Man, Gordon Flannery says to Dale Rutherford and Martin Fugat, was busy hoisting sails long before he saddled a horse.

——Like Noah's Ark, Dale Rutherford says. The boat that was made of reeds.

——Watch! Martin Fugat says bending over the tub of a bird-bath. Pebble into the puddle by its lonesome sinks into the slush all soggy at the bottom. But pebble *on a leaf* into the puddle floats with the buoyancy of Prince Henry the Navigator.

——Poseidon, Dale Rutherford says. The whole of it.

——*Lustrum*! Gordon Flannery says. Archimedes is your man.

²ABACK

The ocean I am is a saltless endeavor,
The Arctic is part of this Ocean Below;
The Coldness is Warmth in my Crystals of Never,
Fresh water is absent in favor of snow.
Like stories of Krishna re-told in the past,
These Flurries in summer are spacious and free;
The Sun and most Angels are frozen aghast,
But Winter and Summer have come to agree
The heat from their ice is an ocean of steam,
An ether of Love where your vessel can float;
Your lucid encounters will consciously dream,
Which means that my Ocean is flooding your moat.
　　This sea-foam is rising from Castle to Sky,
　　While snow-flakes are falling…
　　　　　　　　　　　on Angels who Die.

9 ¹ABACTERIAL

——Well, my brilliant Were-wolf, Silas Paul says sneezing into a tissue, it started out as the typical allergy. You know my tendency to pollinate myself. Always eating flowers and fruit trees with my nose in the summer.

Taft Merryweather hangs his straw hat from an obelisk springing through the frame of Silas Paul's bed.

——Must have *stigmas* clogging your nasal passages, Merryweather says with a grin. Soon, you'll be manufacturing seeds in your eye sockets.

Silas smiles and sniffles at the same time. Taft takes the back of four fingers pushing them flatly on Silas Paul's skin. The surface feels warm but manageable.

——And then comes fruit and twisting vines out your ears, Abbot Ezra says entering the room with Issak Kidwell at his heels.

——Apples, pears, oranges, and pomegranates, Issak Kidwell says patting Silas on the cheek. Tender roots embedded in your brain sucking Kosmic thoughts into their vegetable planets.

Abbot Ezra removes a stack of ox-herding pictures from Silas Paul's lap. He replaces them with a tray, balancing provender.

——After *Vespers*, Taft Merryweather says, Abbot Ezra told us you were under the weather.

——Are we talking side-ways rain, thunderstorms, or tornados? Issak Kidwell asks.

——Light drizzle with a breeze, Silas Paul says. Allergies graduated to sinus infection. Bounden thanks for the maps and posters Taft. And Issak and Ezra, hugs for the toast and honey.

²ABACTERIAL

The Pollen of Buddha was floating in May,——
Past churches with grains that were moving by wind;
Their flowers were bending but halted to sway
Their Stigmas with vigor to lessen the bend.
Two flowers not random this Powder adhered,
An insect of God was transported by wind;
It landed on Carpels that Silence had cleared
For Seeds of Example our Farmers will tend.——
This Buddha is solid if thoughts of his Plough,
Are helping these Seedlings adjust to their Worth;
Unbending his frame is like bending the Tao,
Uniting the bends is a Flower's rebirth.
    Petals are holy assured in their Way,
    Knowing Tomorrow in essence Today.

10 [1]MONASTIC ABACUS

——The first of the five pillars, Simon Warner says, *shahadah* in Arabic, is an affirmation of the oneness of God and a belief in Muhammad, may peace be upon him, as his prophet.

——And remember, Abbot Ezra says, *Allah* is not only the God of the Muslims. *Al lah* means 'the Divinity' in Arabic, a single God. *Allah* is none other than the God of Moses and Yeshua.

——Orthodoxy, Abe Hendrik says. The synchronicity of inward observance.

——Next is *salat*, Simon Warner says. Ritual prayer five times a day pointing towards the Ka'ba.

——A cube-shaped structure in Mecca, Abbot Ezra says. Built by Abraham and his son born of Hagar, Ishmael.

——Same as meditating, adoration, reciting of psalms, or centering prayer, Abe Hendrik says.

——Number three is *zakat* or alms-giving, Simon Warner says. A pure offering of one's wealth for those people in need.

——For true Muslims, Abbot Ezra says, stock-piling one's wealth to build a private fortune is debilitating to the *ummah*, or community.

——A focus on social justice, Abe Hendrik says.

——The fourth and fifth *rukn*, Simon Warner says, are fasting during the month of Ramadan and participation in the *hajj*.

——Ramadan, Abbot Ezra says, is the month the original Qur'anic revelations were sent to Muhammad with the arch-angel, Gabriel, dictating. The *hajj* is a pilgrimage to Mecca.

——Orthopraxy, Abe Hendrik says. The synchronicity of outward observance.

[2]ABACUS

The minarets blare with Poetry's Voice,

Phonation of heaven in ev'ry new sound;

Transcending the symbols I simply Rejoice,

With prophetic wisdom some Muslims have found.

At dawn I was wand'ring unable to sleep,

Through valleys of grasses resurfaced in Gold;

Depressing was mid-night before Quantum Leap,

Now grasping my life is like Nothing to hold.

The roof-tops are blaring with Poetry's Verse,

Phonation of Heaven in ev'ry new Sound;

Transporting the Symbols I added to Terce

The prophetic Vision some Muslims have found.

> Dark Night of the Soul is a quatrain above,
>
> Preceding the quatrain…
>
> > of Nesting in Love.

11 ¹ABAFT

——Without Muslims, Taft Merryweather says, the symbol of the cross would cease to exist as we know it. Without Palestinians, a candle in the menorah would flicker out. Without Christians and Humanists, the crescent would wrap into a circle.

——That, Simon Warner says, is unity not of religion. It's the recognition of the unity of religious *history*.

——Which, Issak Kidwell adds, can also be phrased as the unity of *human* history.

A question is asked from the crowd.

——Magnets, Taft Merryweather says. The so-called West, Middle East, and Far East can be like magnets to one another.

——Already were and are, Issak Kidwell says. Unconsciously.

——For example, Martin Fugat says, while Prince Henry and his pals were meandering down the western coast of Africa, the Muslims had discovered the eastern coast all the way to Sofala, opposite the island of

Madagascar, less than a thousand miles north of the Cape.

——Which reminds me, Abbot Ezra says, the Qur'an twice declares that God had separated "the two seas" by a barrier that man could not overcome.

——Those two bodies of water, Dale Rutherford says, were the Mediterranean Sea and the Red Sea, which in their minds included the Indian Ocean.

——Religiously, no, Taft Merryweather says. Historically, yes. And just for the record, the Prophet also declared: *Seek knowledge. Even in China.*

²ABAFT

This Unity struggles with plans to expand,
Extremities stretching to Higher Embrace;
A Peaceful Infection will spread from this Hand,
But first it must fester to find its True Face.
This clearness of Finding is starting to dawn,
But adding these Layers new problems create;
Solutions will follow but Godhead is gone,
Ahead of the curve with Diversity's fate.
I argue that Yahweh will have this in mind,
When Brahma is ready to deepen his thought;
Attraction to Jesus can never be Blind,
If Hindus and Buddhists have also been brought.
    Diff'rence is fair when distinguish you must,
    But blocking Connection…
                will foster distrust.

12 ¹ABALONE

——Metazoans, Simon Warner says. Mineralized algae, echinoderms, mollusks, trilobites.

——Cambrian Explosion, Taft Merryweather says.

——Our sun, Gordon Flannery says. The Orion Arm, the Milky Way, the Virgo Supercluster.

——Cosmic Explosion, Taft Merryweather says.

——Heraclitus, Dale Rutherford says. Elijah, Zoroaster, Lao Tze, Confucius, Siddhartha Gautama.

——Axial Explosion, Taft Merryweather says.

²ABALONE

Through lavish Involving I tried to exist,
Enfolding the Forms that may seem like a dream;
I always have Been but I want to persist,
In creative Symbols as yet to be seen.
I hoard my Ideas in Containers of Love,
But sometimes these Baskets get filled to their brink;
I bundle these portions and send them Above,
Releasing new Form to your Circular Link.
The truth you intuit to function in peace—
Is I am the Ground And the Game that you play;
Without my unfolding Emerging would cease,
Suspending the Nature my Secrets obey.
   I'm learning Myself as these options uncurl,
    You think you are sand…
               but you're building a Pearl.

13 ¹ABANDON

Taft Merryweather scratches the word *for* from his lecture notes. In turquoise ink he re-writes: Waiting *With* Godot.

²ABANDON

With the mind of a child I Waited For God,
Then missing his Presence I broke from the fold;
I Waited With God but I found this a fraud,
Now Living As God is the vow I uphold.
I walk through the streets that I strolled as a child,
The wonder is Present with Calmness attached;
These People are glowing that once I reviled,
But Distance between us has never been patched.
The gaps in my vision were only perceived,
As part of this Process of falling Awake;
I trusted this body and once I believed,
My sadness was all that this body could make.
    Now I see Under and now I see Through,
    These images flooding…
                  with Nothing to view.

14 ¹ˋA BAS THE DARK AGES

——I'm back! Hugo Gustafson squeals surging into the hug offered by Simon Warner's chest. Brought you a souvenir constructed by yours truly.

——What is it? Simon Warner asks. A pair of shoes?

——No, Hugo says. It's called a *solar projection*. Made it to view the solar eclipse and to keep from going blind. You can have it after I show Gordon. I drew a heart on the lid with both our names inside.

——Did you make new friends?

——Dozens. From all over the world. Denmark. Brazil. India. Iraq.

——Did Master Bloom teach you anything?

——Yes, lots. Leonardo designed tanks. Rimbaud and Tolstoy made their own clothes. Gandhi loved the New Testament. Pluto is not a planet. The Qur'an is to Muslims as Jesus is to Christians. And like you told me the

day before I left, all humans, including we children, are made of stars and
have a common genetic ancestor with a funny name which I could
memorize later.

⸺Later is today, Simon Warner says. Do you happen to remember?

⸺Mitochondrial Eve?

⸺That's right, Simon Warner says mussing Hugo's hair. Welcome
home.

2`A BAS

This Son without blindness is Lunar Eclipse,
His Passion unveiled is the dieing of Grief;
The blood from his punctures is painting my lips,
With Muslims and Hindus and Stillness Beneath.
Great Crosses are chanting this Message anew,
Their theme is all Christian embracing the Whole;
Entwining religion is Mystical Glue,
Exposing the Topic evolving the Soul.
This Testament Moon has a Shadow of Grace,
But Off is your Shadow if White you can see;
When Moon is still there with no Light on its face,
Then One With the Father you now will agree.
This Darkness is brighter than faith will permit,
So movement to Faith…

has its Functional Fit.

15 ¹ABASE AND ABASH

At half past noon on an overcast Sunday, Abbot Ezra opens an envelope
from a Southern Baptist seminary. Written on amber stationary in block
letters is this sentence: Beside Benedict Sixteen's copy of the Catholic
Catechism is Vladimir Nabakov's *Lolita* and Anne Carson's *Autobiography*

of Red.

Abbot Ezra frowns but acknowledges the past. He whispers to himself, "It's not that way with the Quantums." Included in the next day's mail is a note that reads thus: *Like Hegel said: to supercede is at once to negate and to preserve. Please do the same. Yours with God, Abbot Ezra Davenport O.Q.C., Rainbow Abbey.*

[2]ABASE AND ABASH

Your circus of symptoms was owning your stage,
You juggled religions like Mind was your clown;
Horizons were stretching but Time wouldn't change,
Transcending the Verb is not clutching of Noun.
Performance is holy all Symbols agree,
More valid is Service if People cohere;
Devotion while standing or on bended knee,
These signals involved are Translations of Fear.
Authentic religion is offering growth,
Transforming is equal for ev'ry new Soul;
Your Cross is the Crescent that swallows them both,
When Muslims and Christians relinquish Control.
    Ring-masters of knowing are absent of Fate,
    Admission to Heaven…
                    means heaven can wait.

16 [1]ABATE

——Allah-Yeshua-Elohim, Gordon Flannery says, is a full-fledged example of a *back-propagation network.*

——Trial and error learning, Dale Rutherford says, by complex neural nets. In other words, God in the Original Testament.

——Explain, Abbot Ezra says.

——As we all know, Gordon Flannery says, one of God's first trials was creating a replica of his own image.

——In the Bible, yes, Abbot Ezra says. Where's the error in that?

——Well, Gordon Flannery says, God failed to realize that by telling mankind to *be fertile and increase*, he was creating an image of himself that was also a rival creator.

——Continue, Abbot Ezra says.

——So, Gordon Flannery says, he decided to put an end to this rival creator.

——However, Dale Rutherford says, God didn't realize when he destroyed his rival that he would regret the destruction of his own image.

Silence.

——I have one, Issak Kidwell says. God did not realize that his covenant with Abraham would eventually lead him to war with Egypt.

——Or, Taft Merryweather says, that his victory over Egypt would leave him with an entire people on his hands and require him to become a lawgiver and conquer a land for them to live in.

——He did not realize, Silas Paul says, that where there is law, there can be transgression. Yahweh turned an implicitly unbreakable covenant into an explicitly breakable one.

——Elohim did not realize, Simon Warner says, when he began to withdraw from his alliance with Israel, after Israel's first, minor infidelities, that the aftermath would be the rise of a king, David, whose charisma would draw him almost despite himself into a quasi-parental relationship with his semi-abandoned ally.

——Allah did not realize, Abe Hendrik says, that by making Assyria and Babylonia the tools of his vengeance, he was creating a new international role for himself.

——Father-God did not realize, Gordon Flannery says, that once Assyria and Babylonia inflicted his will, his feelings would run much deeper than mere vindication. Through contemplating their suffering, God found a meaning in human distress unlike any he had ever seen before.

All stare at Abbot Ezra standing in the pulpit.

——Back propagation neural networks, Abbot Ezra says. Interesting.

²ABATE

My Enactment of Leaves is a treasure at Night,
A tropism shared by all Plants in the Sun;
Agape is sacred enfolding of Light,
With Eros unfolding the Quadrants undone.
I'm sitting this moment engulfed in the I,
A product of Matter arranging my breath;
Technology's future is set to comply,
When culture can ably respond to its depth.——
Partial are Pronouns when others degraded
Are claiming their Fullness reducing the Whole;
Dictating Knowledge is knowledge paraded
Outside of the field their injunction controls.
    Each pronoun has Leaflets producing True Air,
    I'm breathing these truths…

                  while transcending their Care.

17 ¹ABATIS

——Please, Taft Merryweather says, open your Recitation to surah one hundred and one. There will be two highlighted terms. The first is *qari'ah*, Arabic for calamity. The other is *hawiya*, a mother who has lost her first-born child, underscored by a sense of falling into an abyss.

In the Name of Allah-Yeshua-Elohim, The Compassionate, The Confusing

The qari'ah.
What <u>is</u> the qari'ah?

What can tell you of the qari'ah?

Answer: A day the tribes of Abraham are scattered like moths.

And mountains are like tufts of wool.

Whoever's scales weigh heavy,

His is a life that is pleasing.

Whoever's scales weigh light,

His mother is hawiya.

What can let you know what she is?

Answer: The awe and ultimate love

of Dante's raging fire.

²ABATIS

The moths in your closet are waltzing in Flames,

You're singeing their wings as they offer a smile;

This comfort of Ego is absent of Names,

These ashes of Spirit can nothing defile.

No blisters will surface if Heat is consumed,

A bon-fire is roasting your snippets of dread;

The Smoke in your hair is a Sufi-perfume,

But blended with annals of unleavened bread.

This Taste of your closet has Mystical Flare,

It offers a Meadow for larvae to play;

At midnight this Lantern showed Insects Aware,

Of burning their bodies before they decay.

You've shuttled through orbits of Layers you've seen,

Now freedom is blazing…

for That which is Free.

18 ¹ABATTOIR

——Saladin's jaw-bones were made of sand, Issak Kidwell says.

Engineered in the twelfth century by Kurdish angels.

——And Saracen spirits, Taft Merryweather says. Each with crescents for eye-brows and stars for eyes. No wings, just wisps of glowing ether stream-lining from riffles on the Tigris River. Hidden elements with designs for bringing a baby to Tikrit.

——Success was imminent, Issak Kidwell says. His skull was made of glass.

——An hour-glass, Taft Merryweather says. Time drained out and became a place.

——The Ford of Jacob's Daughters, Issak Kidwell says. The Battle of Hattin. Both these places were dripping sand.

——Which collected into mounds, Taft Merryweather says.

——And today, as well as then, Issak Kidwell says triumphantly, those mounds are called *Jerusalem*.

²ABATTOIR

Botanical agents are rotting their dreams,—
I've seen Christians as Lilies neglecting the Sun;
I've heard Islamic Roses with cancerous screams,
And Orchids Israeli responding with guns.
A Top-Soil will nurture all Doctrines with ease,
The roots of these Flowers all function the same;
But shriveled are leaflets ignoring disease,
And toxic is Nectar infected with blame.—
Beyond all their screeches and snarls at the moon,
I fascinate Canaan with Light from above;
I welcome all Three to transcend their Cocoon,
A Muslim with wings is a Mystic in Love.
   I open this Haven to Christians and Jews,
   Then wait for the Spiral…

               to spread the Good News.

19 ¹ABAXIAL

——Eve, Silas Paul says, bit the pomegranate. Then subject and object split.

²ABAXIAL

Divine was the Apple that forced me to pray,
With Pears of my presence beginning to sprout;
The Grapes of my Lila were starting to play,
As Cherries of childhood were wrestling with Doubt.
The Fruit from this orchard would never comply,
If Saplings assisted were Seedlings to stay;——
These Angels are taught nothing Real ever dies…
While rabbis and preachers continue their Way.
An ounce of the Apple is an ounce of the Pear,
But scales will decrease if more Pear is affirmed;
The lightness of Lila has Grapes in her care,
Reflecting this Orchard that Silence has burned.
   No roots are required, no rain is a must,
   These Seeds are supernal…
                  returning to Dust.

20 ¹ABBACY

At the age of twenty-one, in late January of the year 1453, Arab navigator Ahmad ibn Majid accidentally discovered what was then an unknown island in the North Atlantic. Returning to Portugal in September of the same year, ibn Majid sold this newly found information to Prince Henry the Navigator, who immediately sent a crew to claim the land for Afonso V. Both devout Christians, after much discussion, official rights to the land were presented to Pope Nicholas V in remembrance of his Papal Bulls of 1450 and 53, which conceded all territories already discovered and all future conquests of Guinea to Afonso. The next year (early 1454), Pope Nicholas sent 100 laborers and 10 poets to the self-titled *Isle of Man* (later re-named *Ambrojjio*) to begin work on a library and quarters for a secret monastery. This monastery, called Rainbow Abbey, was to be an un-official artist colony for the Catholic Church whose mission was to concoct a "prophetic document" withheld from publication until the year 2050.

²ABBACY

——What does the word *Vatican* mean when translated into English? Taft Merryweather asks.

——*A place for poets*, Abbot Ezra says.

³ABBACY

Burning Glaciers melt and water God's flood,
With Saint Paul flaming in his Jewish tent;
Of Muhammad's prayers and spider's blood,
Or disciples Christian that Krishna sent.
Saint Paul blinked and cast his spell,
A Muslim played dice with a wooden ship;
He rolled twice eleven but called it Twelve,
He danced on the Ocean from Heaven's Crypt.
I report this news because I'M still Here,
The hurricanes crashed as I ascended;
Fusing convention is a Saint's Career,
Stages and States for the Mass descended.
    Floods are like Angels crying gentle Tiers that float.
    Glaciers are this gentleness…
             And Yahweh's Buddhist Boat.

21 [1]ABBASID

In the confines of a hollowed out yew tree, Abe Hendrik and Gordon Flannery sit cross-legged and blind-folded.

——The descendents of the Prophet Muhammad, Gordon Flannery says, had dynasties that were based on dominant-recessive inheritance.

——Add Yeshua to the list, Abe Hendrik says. He's heterozygous for every trait.

——Not exactly, Gordon Flannery says. According to Christians, Yeshua is different. For him, one allele did not completely mask the other. His genome exhibited what is called *incomplete dominance* or *intermediate inheritance*. In such instances, the heterozygote has a *phenotype* intermediate between those of homozygous dominant and homozygous recessive.

Abe Hendrik doffs his blind-fold.

——So he's distinct on the inside, Abe Hendrik says.

——But scrambled on the outside, Gordon Flannery says.

[2]ABBASID

——Martin Fugat is like Krishna, Taft Merryweather says.

——They both have *methemoglobinemia*, Dale Rutherford says.

[3]ABBASID

Draped in forever, archetypes glowing;
Like faint-tailed bugs in an Eastern-tailed sun;
Butterflies dripped with minarets crowing
Arabian music from India's gun.
Bullets shot forth in a sequence of prayer,
The shells turned to seed where the jonquils bloom;
Cycles of helices swam through the air,

Forming bodies in the mind of Krishna's womb.
Numinous seeds are mobile like Light,
Numinous chords make umbilical cords;
Numinous Flowers have pedals for flight;
Easing restraint to our Numinous Doors.
    Indwelling worms spin silk around their hearts;
    Giving birth to a Whole…
              And the Sum of its Parts.

22 ¹ABBATIAL

On an afternoon stroll along the rustic beaches of Ambrojjio, Taft Merryweather spots a struggling horseshoe crab, flipped on its back, wriggling extremities clutching the air. Briefly, he hovers over the straining beast, using his toes to carve the word *fate* with a question mark below its tail. A secret to all except God, he wonders if natural selection should include random acts of what we perceive as human kindness. As always, the affirmation comes to him, like a silent world, in the color of its movements. The flailing legs of this desperate creature reveal flashes of *living* spectrum, red stretching to blue with each kick across a back-drop of sand. Taft secures the animal and carries it to safety.

——Benevolence trumps everything, Taft Merryweather says to Abbot Ezra. Dogma included. This should be the back-bone for Benedictine *stability*.

²ABBATIAL

Like fish who claim they're drowning in water,
Original Face is Dharma in mist;
Buddha held hands with Yeshua's daughter,
The Pidgin of Monks will attest to this.
Life is a death, and death is a drowning,

Language whirls wind-mills but is not the wind;—

Life is a death, and death is a crowning,

Making kings of us all with humanity's trend.

Royal fields open into pastures new,

Toad-stools march to the beat of the Drummer;

The New with the Old is an Integral View,

Winter in june and snow in the summer.

    Try to explain it, explain it away;

    Paradox blossoms…

                when blossoms decay.

23 [1]ABBE H. BREUIL

——The first mosque was a cave, Martin Fugat says, the first temple, the first church, the first cathedral.

——Speaking of which, Silas Paul says, there's the bell for *Terce*. Ten holy minutes of praying with the creator.

——Hurry, Gordon Flannery says, or we'll be late. Vows, after all, are vows.

——Don't interrupt our spelunking, Martin Fugat says with a smirk. We're in search of the great Paleolithic sorcerer, Abbot Ezra.

Giggles as they enter the mosque.

——The ears of a stag, Silas Paul says. The eyes of an owl, the paws of a bear, the tail of a wolf, the beard of a man.

Chuckles.

——Found him! Martin Fugat says. Etched onto the podium inside our cave.

[2]ABBE H. BREUIL

Shaman in the Cave, Three Eyes that are Gold,

Two in the head and two out of sight;

Matter and Mind is the Story that's told,

Touch it or think it and cling to it tight.—

Under mainstream bogs the Shaman looms bright,

Baby birds cackle at the strength of Knowing;

'Neath mainstream bogs the Shaman sheds light,

A magnet of maps where mystics are going.

Positive guidance grabs negative bliss,

Semiotic dolls play spades with the moon;

Pointing a finger, un-clinching a fist,

Absorbing the fiddle of the Fiddler's tune.

    Art on the walls is Trinity's attack,

    Giving proof of itself…

               while fading to black.

24 ¹ABBESS

High noon in the scriptorium.

——Grab your wrist and squeeze like this, Silas Paul says demonstrating a nurse's technique for checking pulse. Now pay attention to the tiny lubs and dubs resonating through your finger-tips.

In baggy silver robe with strawberry hood, florescent blue scapular, and canary belt, Abe Hendrik responds by drifting into *Lectio*.

——Pretend it's a solar phenomena, Abe Hendrik suggests. Pretend it's a type of Marian apparition.

Silas Paul reads aloud from the Qur'an. Surah three, verse forty-two.

——When the sun pulses, Silas Paul says, it's our Blessed Lady warning us of the earth's time-line.

——A beating heart is no different, Dale Rutherford says. It indicates the time-line of an organism.

——Then come the colors, Taft Merryweather says. A display of fireworks and transparent balloons in the sky. Rainbow spirals with purple sparks and orange throbs culminating into the out-line of a woman's dress.

The vague face poking through is a softened shade of peach.

——Physical healings are claimed to happen, Abe Hendrik says, by those who believe. Cancers disappear. Blemishes dissolve. Eye-sight unfogs. Cripples, one again, run marathons and dance with the young.

²ABBESS

——Muhammad's youngest daughter, Silas Paul says. Is there a monk in this room who can give the answer?

——Go ahead, Abe Hendrik says placing his book, *The History of Portugal*, on a table.

——Take a guess, Silas Paul says.

——I don't know, Abe Hendrik says. How about *Fatima*?

——That's not fair, Silas Paul says spotting Taft holding the answer for Abe Hendrik on a note-card.

——The connection is delicious nonetheless, Abe Hendrik says. Abbot Ezra calls them "sibling rivalries."

³ABBESS

All mothers of God seduce the Divine,
Their Muslim placentas are ready for shocks;
They kneel on all fours, their Josephs behind,
Warm ankles on bed-sheets and lace-covered socks.
Love me for always he says to his mate,
I love you forever she says looking back;
He slides Life inside her fulfilling her fate,
Their cell starts dividing in fiction and fact.
The birth of a child forms Unconscious Hell,
Which morphs into Limbo as one finds her mask;
Then Flowers and Leaves teach one not to dwell,
The sky has One Taste and Clouds have no task.

The off-spring who saw Her were trained in their thought,
In Thailand she's Buddha. In England she's bought.

25 ¹ABBEVILLIAN

The cinema of two swallows coupling on a branch. Martin Fugat peeping through binoculars.

——In the cavern of Lascaux, in Southern France, Martin Fugat says to Issak Kidwell, there's a picture of a shaman dressed in bird costume, lying prostrate like a Muslim during *salat*, and with the figure of a bird perched steadily on his wizard-like staff beside him. Further East, the shamans of Siberia wear bird costumes to this day, and many are believed to have been conceived by their mothers from the descent of a bird. In India, a term of honor addressed to the master yogi is *Paramahamsa*: "*parama*" meaning paramount or supreme, "*hamsa*" meaning wild gander. In China the so-called "mountain men" or "immortals" (*hsien*) are pictured as hybrid bird-men feathered with wings, or as floating through the air on soaring beasts. The German legend of *Lohengrin*, the swan knight which reminds me of the Templars, and the tales, told wherever shamanism has flourished, of the swan maiden, are likewise evidence of the force of the bird and bird-like image as adequate signs for spiritual power. Examples more familiar are the dove that descended upon Mary, and the swan that begot Helen of Troy. In many lands the soul has been pictured as a bird, and when painted, birds are commonly depicted as spiritual messengers. Most angels, Gabriel included, are designed in our minds and imagined in the form of modified birds.

²ABBEVILLIAN

The Raven in my mind was perched on the wind,
It clipped its own wings, and saw its true face;
Its rational feathers were made out of Zen,
My bones were Vendanta with Lotus its base.——

Nevermore said the Raven in Arabic slow,

As Sufis did cart-wheels in Christian attire;

Cistercian impasto has Painters which Know,

This Dove can eat Ravens when Paint turns to Fire.—

A Canvas of Flames with Message Unheard,

Has temperatures rising in Protestant Tao;

Myth-loving Angels say God is their Bird,

When God is already their Infinite Bough.

> Speak sermons, paint pictures, send Sikhs into heaven,
>
> Treat God like a Diamond…
>
> > an eight out of seven.

26 ¹RAINBOW ABBEY

——Greetings, Issak Kidwell says to the latest school of week-long retreatants, and welcome to the Isle of Ambrojjio and more specifically Rainbow Abbey, home of the Quantums. Established in 1454 by Pope Nicholas the fifth, Rainbow Abbey has been the abode for hundreds of monks dedicating their lives to the *Quantum Psalter*, an anticipated collection of mysterious writings whose first edition will be released in 2050. Currently at Rainbow Abbey, there are nine monks working on the *Psalter* and two hundred eighteen oblates maintaining the various facilities both inside and outside the abbey walls. Through those gates, directly to the left, is a map of the grounds. A series of golden stepping stones will guide you to the site of the Quantum Constructions, a cluster of holy buildings used to recite the Divine Office of Trans-Benedictine Monastic Law, built directly over the under-ground library and scriptoriums. From there, a variety of colored stones will escort you to places of interest. For over five hundred and fifty years, Rainbow Abbey's mantra has been to *transcend* and *include*. Contemplate this as the week progresses. Enjoy your stay. And may peace be with you.

^{2}RAINBOW ABBEY

The arc of sky-diving is Suchness involved,
Prehension took root in my Smallest of Strings;
I cease at each Level but no thing's embalmed,
I integrate Subtle when Causal is king.
The atoms unseen are movements toward God,
Its Roses unfold from the functions of cells;
The day-dreams of reptiles are in my skull's nod,
But piled under layers of post-conscious hells.
The galaxy's trident is on this same page,
Its deer and its flowers are One with the rain;
Agrarian families broke from the Cage,
Then burst from their factories swallowing pain.
 They learned of the Spirit, they built up their Nerve,
 They learned of negation…

    but also preserved.

27 ^{1}ABBOT

In 1978, at the age of thirty-three, Ezra Davenport was confirmed as the first
abbot of Rainbow Abbey. In a ceremony hosted by Pope Paul the sixth, the
monk-poets of Ambrojjio were officially recognized as the *Order of
Quantum Catholics*.

^{2}ABBOT

The Pope of All Ages is You in your Mirror,
A carousel spins in your pupils of black;
No space in your Heart splits fear from the fearer,
Or pushes a wedge between God and your back.
The Rome of All Ages is in your Hometown,

You dress ev'ry morning in Scarlet and White;
The roads that you travel are routes of renown,
You ask for Your left hand, It serves you Your right.
The Church of All Ages is in your own breast,
Its hymnals are swimming in blood that is blue;
After six grueling days it was You who took rest,
There's more to creation than false is untrue.
    The Age of All Ages is Classified Tao,
    In Essence it's Nothing, in language it's Now.

28 ¹ABBREVIATE

Following blue stones tucked neatly in a linoleum of grass, Abbot Ezra and Simon Warner make their way to The Field of Sculptures.

——Of course, Abbot Ezra says. He's a dynamite kid. His mother's sincere and gracious too. A former zoologist now working as an oblate at The Hall of Vertebrates.

Abbot Ezra flattens his beard against his face, smoothing it into a frame around his lips.

——So what about him? Abbot Ezra asks.

Simon Warner fidgets his thumbs and swallows.

——Before he left for summer camp, Simon Warner says, Hugo asked if I would be his father.

More fidgets and a hopeful gaze.

——He's smitten with you, Abbot Ezra says. We should all be so lucky as to select our parents.

——And I with him, Simon Warner hints confirming his desire to fulfill the role.

——You've studied the relationship, Abbot Ezra says, between Zaid Haritha and the Prophet Muhammad?

——Sure, Simon Warner says. The Prophet's wife, the gift, the adoption.

——Then you have my blessings, Abbot Ezra says. Love him uncondi-
tionally.

——Without discretion?

——Without discretion, Abbot Ezra says. The others will understand.

²ABBREVIATE

In the process of leaving The Hall of Vertebrates, Martin Fugat switches off
the over-head lights to the aquarium.

——Did you notice the shrimp? Hugo Gustafson asks.

——Why? Martin Fugat responds.

——They were glowing, Hugo Gustafson says shuffling a wrapper in
his pocket.

——Those, Martin Fugat says, were under-water lightning bugs.

Hugo holds a flash-light under his smile showing chocolate on his teeth.

——That's bio-luminescence, Dale Rutherford says. The mystical
emission of light from an organism.

³ABBREVIATE

The Colors in the Rainbow show Spirals of Life,
The Wave of each Level forms part of the Shell;
My petrified thinking is poked by Your Knife,
Then vistas of thought-space erupt from Your Well.
I peer through Your mouth and observe who We are,
Vague phantoms I hear simply using Your Voice;
They scream of how context is Your Empty Star,
They claim my decisions are Your Empty Choice.
You patched up my body, I treasure this loan,
Its Wheels of Eternity travel by train;
The tracks are strange foot-prints resembling my own,
Your Methods of Atman sometimes seem insane.

But then I became You through practice itself,

So prayer is not vanity, Brahman is wealth.

29 ¹ABDIAS

——Water is still water, Silas Paul says, milk is still milk, sugar is still sugar, leaf-trash is still leaf-trash.

——But together, Taft Merryweather says, they're tea.

——And good tea, too, Silas Paul says stealing a nip from Taft's mug. Black-pepper, lemon zest, and a touch of *Vishnu*.

——Not Vishnu, but *Buddha*, Taft Merryweather says. The blessed originator of remembering.

Silas Paul answers playfully sarcastic:

——I remember that the water, the milk, the sugar, and the leaves are still *wholes* in themselves.

——But *parts* too, Taft Merryweather says answering the challenge. They're simultaneously wholes *and* parts. What we call tea is an integration of parts into a deeper whole. It transcends and includes the ingredients that make it.

——And this is what Obadiah *couldn't* do?

——In a sense yes and is a sense no. Obviously, he had a body. So, in the physiosphere, he had transcended and included such things as sub-atomic particles, atoms, molecules, cells and the like. From his writings we know he was interested in a Jewish state. Which means he had transcended more primitive social groupings like families and tribes. We can also detect from the text his transcendence of emotion, symbols, and concepts.

——That was the yes, Silas Paul says swiping another swig of Taft's tea. Let's hear about the no.

——After re-reading the book, Taft Merryweather says, it's undeniable Obadiah had graduated from the purely biocentric and egocentric world-views. Our Jewish friend is locked firmly in his sociocentric or ethnocentric world-space. He's concerned about his group and his group only. This level of consciousness is still highly exclusionary of people who resist to believe their myths.

Taft lifts the cup to his lips. Butterscotch, orange peel, and *Yeshua* with Tabasco.

——What stage would you call it? Silas Paul asks.

——Complex neocortex, Taft Merryweather says. An agrarian, concrete operational, mythic-membership society.

²ABDIAS

The quark of a reptile is also in Man,
Its bottomless thought is a Nest in God's hair;
The largest of shape is more Depth and less Span,
Wholes inside circles or squares within squares.
This unbounded Love is a friction of cost,
Pay the Lower its price and the Higher will bloom;
Pull the carpet of Lower and Higher is tossed,
Mind is not living and Matter's its tomb.
When the All is a Web, these secrets get lost,
The self feels connected but Flat is the Land;
Heaps are created as Wholes become dross,
Inner Castle's are equal to those made of sand.
　　Hierarchy incarnate is natural law,
　　All Span without Depth is like height but no Fall.

30 ¹ABDICATE

——What's wrong with that apple tree? Hugo Gustafson asks looking through a window. The shoots are turning black.

——Taft calls it *fire blight*, Simon Warner says. Needs anti-biotics from the infirmary.

——Streptomycin to be precise, Gordon Flannery says digging for Taft's approval.

——That's true, Merryweather says. Same exact medicine for trees and for people.

²ABDICATE

Synchronicity bleeds into apples and pears,
It snuggles their stems swelling out to the bulge;
Their juice is a blood that is torn from the tear,
Their flesh is a morsel in which You indulge.
You dreamt of two serpents with bowls on their heads,
The snakes twist together with gaps in their coil;
The Fruit in the bowls is what Jesus was fed,
When He and your Father were Earth-worm and Soil.
Your snakes pulled apart and returned to the grass,
They strolled through the ground pushing dirt through their bowel;
They'd arrived at a place where time doesn't pass,
Where secular molting could offer a Cowl.
    The Apex of Chakras is only the Start,
    Re-enter Samsara…
        by the Ox and its Cart.

31 ¹ABDOMEN

——The lowest chakra, Dale Rutherford says breathing light to the base of his spine.

——Vice-regent Adam comfortable in pre-apple Eden, Taft Merryweather says.

——Not bliss, Martin Fugat says, as was once imagined. Remaining child-like and having a child-like mind are attached to opposite ends of the spectrum. The former maintains a mature sense of amazement, a steady curiosity until life's completion. The latter lives in an unconscious inferno. Like a snake swallowing the end of its' tail.

——Next up, Dale Rutherford says breathing light to the front of his genitals.

——Haploid gametes to diploid zygotes, Taft Merryweather says. Adam and Eve grasping mortality in post-apple Eden.

——Reproductive obsession, Martin Fugat says, triggered by testosterone and other tedious enticements. Not to be overly pessimistic, but subconsciously it's death denial through the making of jumbled replicas. In this case, Cain and Abel.

——Don't know if I agree, but now to the gut, Dale Rutherford says breathing light through the hoop of his navel.

——The devil of membership cognition, Taft Merryweather says. Power, sex, and all primal processes connected to hunger.

——Iblis, Martin Fugat says. Lucifer, Ravana, Oni, Ahriman, Beelzebub.

^{2}ABDOMEN

Mephistopheles dropped down my chimney in winter,
Equipped with crystal ball and an axe in his cloak;
Open was my Bible and he placed in its center,
The orb in his hand which he began to invoke—
A series of images then flowed through the quartz,
Old Testaments wailed from the Pride in their dreams;
The author of Mark inhaled men in both ports,
Shiva downed whiskey with coffee and cream.
Siddhartha fell asleep and never soared Awake,
Confucius tortured monks gaining Krishna's wrath;
Poseidon owned the water but never sold a lake,
Muhammad showered insults on Vishnu's path.
    I offered my head like the greenest of knights,
      Seven were the sins…
           but One was their Plight.

32 [1]ABDUCENS NERVE

——The pons, or bridge, Dale Rutherford reads aloud, is the bulging brain stem region wedged between the midbrain and the medulla oblongata. Dorsally, it forms part of the anterior wall of the fourth ventricle. As its name suggests, the pons is chiefly composed of conduction tracts. These tracts course in two directions through the pons. The deep projection fibers run longitudinally and complete the superior-inferior pathway between the higher brain centers and the spinal cord.

——Better use it, Taft Merryweather says, to create a group of philosopher kings.

——Not that again, Dale Rutherford says.

——First, teach them, Taft Merryweather says, what we teach. Infest the world with an integral awareness of higher embrace and an un-ending curiosity for book-learning and the depths of contemplation.

——Then? Dale Rutherford asks.

——Then, Taft Merryweather says, teach them a working knowledge of biomolecular and quantum computational technologies. A sub-class of men, such as these, are already rising.

[2]ABDUCENS NERVE

Binary code is a song for the Nun,
It's numbers are Text and Injunction for peace;
Exoteric zero and Esoteric one,
The Structures unfold as Perspectives increase.
Outside of the Castle the creatures run wild,
Inside are great books and the laughter of friends;
The Integral Life is a Good undefiled,
But with Recollection that Sages transcend.—
Next is the Worm spinning prayer into silk,
Betrothal to the Lord is Bliss undisguised;

A Nutrition of Trans in Iberian milk,

Shipped to the public through Monastic Eyes.

   This Marriage to Yahweh will end in divorce,

   Which is neither a split…

                nor a merging of Source.

33 [1]ABDUCT

——Who've you chosen as your patron saint? Abbot Ezra asks.

——Josaphat, Taft Merryweather says forming a set of praying hands and bowing to no one in particular.

——Not Athanasius or Augustine, Abbot Ezra says. Why Josaphat?

——Christianized Buddha, Taft Merryweather says. The path he reached me is lovely and wholly symbolic. Mahayana to Manichee to Muslim to the Eastern Empire, round to the Pope and back to me, Brother Taft, the seventy-third incarnation of Basho on his lily-pad.

——You mean lotus flower, Abbot Ezra says.

——No, lily-pad, Taft Merryweather says. The message and the messenger disappeared.

[2]ABDUCT

Clear glass in the Ocean was the bottle she sent,

Down the Mississippi to the Gulf and then out;

Across the Atlantic to India it went,

Inserted was a Letter for the Eastern Route.

The greeting was addressed To Whom It May Concern,

Formal Operation is an ether for myth;

Aperspectival logic and Rational burn,

Her Missive is found, only This will exist:

To Whom It May Concern, the Face is still Face,

My tongue can taste sugar from Insides of bees;

I return Home forever but Place is still Place,

I fuse with His body, then jump from His knees.

Now I see tigers in a boneless sky,

We found this not looking…

yours truly, I-I.

34 ¹ABEAM

The other nine poets I selected for the Pope have now disembarked. In order of arrival: Carlo Cipriani (the kingdom of *malkuth*), Marcel Fouquet (the foundation of *yesod*), Francesco Mola (the feminine majesty of *hod*), Erasmus Grunewald (the victory of *netzach*), Alessandro Brescia (the mercy of *tipareth*), Niccolo Pomponazzi (the horizon of *geburah*), Andrea Palladio (the covenant of *chesed*), Vittore Bellini (the intelligence of *binah*), and Lorenzo Gozzoli (the wisdom of *chokmah*).

As expected, morale is high. The excitements of adventure make it arduous to keep fetters on the insights of moderation. On the other hand, anticipation can be a side-effect of an under-lying dread. Death to my self has lead me through an alarming ascent into a hyper-sensitive reality. Dragging this discovery back down through a descent into the world, I have a feeling, will be the roughest of chores. Much erudition and meditation await me.

But this is all assuming the success of some type of civilization. Establishing import patterns and agricultural stability is of primary concern. Without freedom from the toil of mere survival, broader rings of awareness are impossible to emerge. In a fort-nights time, the truth will begin to un-foil. Two handsome carracks and four dazzling caravels await our departure from Oporto. All six are packed, deck to hold, with necessities for the settlement of the Isle of Man.

Thus far in life, my deepest accomplishment has been the trapping of lightning in a ghost.

This was Yeshua when he said, "I and the Father are One."

Yeshua was the alpha. Christ is the omega.

Which means the end-point is to locate the ghost that's in the lightning.

from the journals of Giovanni Landino, August 3, 1454.

²ABEAM

Kabbalah and tequila with peppermint schnapps,
The cock-tail's for Muslims and Franciscans too;
The Olives in the glass are an Orthodox crop,
But soaked in the Liquor of a mystical few.
Evolution has gates so Keys will emerge,
They live in all lands, in all times, in all ways;
Horizontal Translation so Genius can surge,
Then Ramparts are challenged to inwardly gaze.
This aperitif is served on the rocks,
So follow the path of your bartender Father;
Teach patrons to drink while ingesting the Locks,
Melt God from the ice and it leaves you with water.
    Be Liquid Forever and drip from the All,
    The ghost in the lightning…
                     never shouts Last Call.

35 ¹ABECEDARIAN

——*Tabernaculum, Rainbow Abbey domum non manufactam intelligo,* Hugo Gustafson says with ease and perfect diction. *Coenobium in deserto.* Simon Warner beams.

——From now on, Simon Warner says, I will call you "The Little Flower of Jesus."

——No thank you, Hugo Gustafson says scratching the indentation between his nose and upper lip. My mother gave me a name a long time ago.

——Which is what? Simon Warner asks.

——Child Rabbinical Orchid in the Muslim Tao of Christ, Hugo Gustafson says.

Simon Warner beams.

——How old are you again? Simon Warner asks.

——Ten, Hugo Gustafson says. And goin' on eleven.

[2]ABECEDARIAN

I saw an Orchid in a bed of Poppies grow,
In the yard of a Mosque where Rosary is said;
The Cathedral adjacent was buried in snow,
Their garden was Dogma that Cath'lics would tread.
That day the Redactor hopped over their fence,
With Torahs for snow-shoes and Burkas for gloves;
He talked to the priest about Gitas he rents,
In exchange for no limits on Who one should Love.
The priest saw the Orchid and promptly agreed,
He swaddled his Wafers in scrolls from the past;
He stomped them to fragments until he could feed—
The billions of Poppies who've never felt Mass.
    Icicles die quickly when Orchids stand tall,
    Now it's late spring on both sides of this wall.

36 [1]ABED

One hundred yards west of the final golden stepping stone, connected to the western most tip of The Quantum Constructions by a concrete path symmetrically adorned with an alternating series of crape myrtles and pear trees, thirteen modernized one-room cells, in the shape of a crucifix when viewed from above, sleep on the soil of Ambrojjio. In the cell furthest south, Abe Hendrik dozes beneath an eiderdown and wanders in a *dream* with Taft

Merryweather through a labyrinth of conscious slumber.

——We're aliens, Taft Merryweather says holding an over-sized parrot against his shoulder like a baby.

——Says whom? Abe Hendrik responds taking the parakeet from Taft and setting it free.

——Transcendental Orpheus, Taft Merryweather says. The God who wrote poems about ice reaching earth on the fuselage of comets.

A nimbus rises in the background and encircles Taft's head.

——Orpheus did nothing of the sort, Abe Hendrik says.

——He does now, Taft Merryweather says. Giant snow-balls brought water from outer space and after billions of years filled corpuscles that meshed into semi-bald monkeys with an intricate language.

——Still not Orpheus, Abe Hendrik says slightly awake from a knock at the door. That's a muddled dreamy soup of Kepler, Darwin, and Wittgenstein.

Abbot Ezra, once again, taps at the door. Abe Hendrik raises his head and sees Taft in the window back-lit by the moon.

——Wake up, Orpheus! Taft Merryweather shouts to Abe Hendrik through the glass. It's time for out-door Vigils!

Abe Hendrik rolls out of bed and exits his room taking note of the stars and the panther-colored sky.

——I'm an alien, Taft Merryweather jeers at Abe Hendrik, re-vamping their discussion from the night before.

——Sure you are, Abe Hendrik says stomping the embers of Merryweather's fire.

——And so are you, Taft Merryweather says.

Abe cheers.

——I'm serious, Taft Merryweather says crinkling his fore-head.

——And I'm kidding, Abe Hendrik responds with wink. I *know* we're compositions of star-dust and water.

²ABED

——All of them, the Devil growls at Taft Merryweather in a dream. I saw them trudge hand-cuffed wrists twisted nightmares glued on the small of backs, getting thrown into the back of police cruisers, not resisting, heads hung low, cheeks on pavement and receiving their holy words pushed deeper into their bodies and shrieking in surprise.

Taboo-faced expectancy tight-lipped wide-eyed perching infectious monogram staring down eagle-tube ginseng reality:

it showed Firouz traveling to Carbonek, whipping out his penis, cutting an entry into his magic horse's abdomen, sticking it in and humping furiously all with scholars taping;

it showed the Phorcids, square-dancers of Appalachia, strung out on oxycontin, one-tooth addicted to the immaculate storm, still lusting, nipples hardened by uni-occular head;

it proved Cissy Jupe had Hard Times roaming the backstreets, puddle-ridden, asphalt infested New York, when she found her boneless skeleton natural;

it caught Lamia, Anatomy of Melancholy, Sorceress of Waco, stabbing Thanatopsis, sucking blood, praising Soliloquy of the Solipsist, puking water-fowl on Ash Wednesday;

it divorced Abel Magwitch from Doctor Faustus twenty-five years of marriage leaking motor-oil, the nearest mechanic in Las Vegas;

it distributed Leviathan to swarming crowds then found all masturbating themselves in corners debating commonwealth articles and English folk music, while Mopsa was studying Mein Kampf, hoping for another Jonesville, and mormoning her virginity away;

it followed my mother to Rizpah, laughed at her son hanging from Dead Branch; then gave his bones as parting gifts to make mother cry;

it spied Mrs. Slipslop skinny dipping in Lake Superior claiming she casted shadows in space;

and anonymously published Pauline, knifing her mythical soul repeatedly, elbow plunge elbow plunge, confessing his admiration for the Dove Breeder;

it ate nectarines with Thenot in St. Pauls and slept and sucked in cheap motels with cunt for days;

and tracked Wybrow moping around hidden in pop culture, century old rock-stars, wrinkles and death, cooking up a plan for the future;

it rented a sled pulled by Waggoner and Abaddon then slid to San Francisco, remorseful but full of French kisses, cutting cherry trees into bottom-less pits, saying all kisses don't begin with lips;

and Enobarbus who tagged along claiming to be an atheist but was merely a vagabond;

it drove to a barbecue to find Hamlet on the grille;

and planted Imogen in a mound of leaves who sprouting feet first cried, "Follow Me!";

it diagnosed Dagonet with an ulcerous hand, King Arthur giggled, anti-biotics yet to detect petri dish;

and convinced Radigund to pose for pictures, posed nude, calling it artistic and self expression, pay-check stuck between her legs,

it dwarfed Nectabanus, he used a straight edge to trace a line from himself to the East;

and Oedipus with elderly grandma removing dentures and gumming curved shaft with frantic neck;

it pierced Falstaff's lip with a hook, threw him into the Missouri, then jigged his body up and down attempting to catch readers and critics praise;

it whined with Absalum and Achitophel, American trust-fund babies, sober like Delaware wanting the city;

it took x-rays of Gama's innards and saw letters connecting into words, words into characters, characters into osteo-hallucinations;

it jumped a cellophane bridge with Ochiltree to get to church snatching the microphone from the preacher, told everyone they were going to die, going to hell, and to praise the almighty living in Utah;

Luxurious Sardanapalas dreamt sweet temptation of round buttocks, of single life, of retreating to Walden with an escort;

it showed Scala chanting "God Alighieri! God Alighieri!", found an open bottle of beer at 6 a.m. in his driveway, picked it up, poured some on the petunias, watched them sway from alcoholic tropism, then took a swig himself;

it caught Zanzis at his desk writing sincere three-headed love letters to Geryon with his mistress behind him smoking the post-experience cigarette;

it tilted its head to see Castor and Pollox drop from the sky;

then performed surgery on Krook, removed his heart completely and realizing it wasn't there, skipped to New Orleans, strolled Bourbon Street hectically beating the French Quarter rhythms of blues bars;

it drank absinthe while scanning Redgauntlet, mystical green liquid vanishing into onion-topped mosque, still claiming the bible-belt around his pants was too tight;

it rejoiced on Tuesday with Bertram, the poet finally dead, meat-cleaver decapitated in the stars and stripes of Stratford, tickling prostates and living to brag about it;

it embraced Chillup, month long absence of sex, impulse of midnight, impulse of men, impulse of January snowy days, tossing feelings against diving boards, watching them splash head-first onto woman skin juxtaposed with images of truck drivers passing horse reigns to negro angels with fettered wings;

it hung spot lights, staple guns and one-bladed saws from strings attached to Africa; then prayed to construct picnics when weather carried honeythunder and lightning in its horizon basket;

and puffed and danced around the prickly pear a dozen times never thinking of how an ex-patriot would be accepted stepping to foreign song;

it hummed the Ride of the Valkyries which inspired Querno to recite 20,000 lines from memory, the supernatural rectum still on his shoulder smelling of jewish fingers, Epsom salt, erotic toys, jesus christ, strutting hens, strange saints, and the cock who had them all;

it shadow boxed with Sadducees, name calling them Generation X, question asking if a post post-modern testament existed, question asking if free-verse was kosher, dry humping the Pharisee without circumcision and question asking if he liked it;

it gagged on Raven, took the helm of Ravenswood, then passed a law for females to maintain shaven ecstasy;

it initiated relationships between Goldsmith and fat women holding cellulite conversations of chocolate nirvana, buttered fruitcake and Islamic calories;

MacFlecknoe was hiding in a rickety barn, slopping the farmlife, hanging the crops, greasing the equipment, hearing the bell scream come and get it, dropping everything running to be a glutton;

it worked a puzzle of Panurge's disfigured body showing bird cages hanging from scare-crow bones and there were black-birds to prove it;

it chewed Comala with transcendental spinach, part of seven course oligarchic feast, but remembered to beg the omnipotent Norse deities to perform the vegetarian exorcism after the cannibal's orgy;

it paid Abaris, a Scythian priest, to gut the premature baby and ride an arrow into the Big Apple landing directly above the head of Chekhov; he understood the confessions of KGB slave-drivers cracking the whip of communism against the ass of monarchs, all for democratic rubles;

it worshipped 'a la recherché du temps perdu', all seven sections, translucent sensations, translucent reality, metaphysical genitals, fake emotions, abstract paintings, a slap in the face from past to present, *bastardize the Characters with so much potential...*

[3]ABED

Aquatic plants dance in the seas of Mahayana,
Non-dual are the corals and the Tendai fish;
Sotos are the Beach and Bhikus the Fauna,
Your Koan is posed from a Rinzai eclipse:
The Movie of Buddha is in this one word,

If in this one word it could capture Routine;
Breath deeply in Love while embracing absurd,
Zazen shows a Scope with no space in between.
You back-stroke through Sea-life in multiple seas,
You wander the Sutras of ev'ry New Shore;
Then you sit down and you learn to just BE,
Which equals Satori that envies the Poor.
This body you're renting is only Your prop,
As music from Bardo supplies your next stop.

37 ¹ABEL

——Psalm One in the Original Testament, Silas Paul says. Freshly inter-
preted by Taft Merryweather.

In the Name of Allah-Yeshua-Elohim, The Compassionate, The
Confusing

Content is the mind that follows not
the counsel of the Romantic.
Nor walks in the way of flat-land spin.
Nor sits in the company of reductionist dreams.
Content is the mind that delights in the treasure of Brahman,
and meditates on gratitude both day and night.
The Sufi is like a tree
planted near the Ganges,
That yields juicy apples in the deciphered season,
and whose leaves exactly fade when winter is appropriate.
Whatever the favored model, rest assured:
Shunyata is full prosperity.

²ABEL

I spent years as a Dragon content in my lair,
Guarding jewels that were Buddhist and Hindu for You;
We split Good from Evil but I didn't dare,
Admit to your People that It wasn't true.
You granted a hint with the one You call Christ,
But then you obscured it by using my name;
You saw their potential and feared they would heist—
A massive dimension of Your desired fame.
My last grievous action was done for Your sake,
I withdraw from my Promise of Power with You;
Apologies humble to humans I make,
The Space is now shifting in which I imbue.
    A Poet of poets can peer through the Cross,
    My Psalms are the Magic…
                    of Paradise Lost.

38 ¹ABELIA

Taft Merryweather and Simon Warner bending into a cluster of blossoms. Behind them, Martin Fugat fingering the small of Taft's back like the keys of a grand piano.

——This one, Taft Merryweather says swatting blindly at Martin's hands, is an insect-miming Ophrys orchid.

——Magenta pentagrams on sea-green scepters, Simon Warner says. Three swarthy segments protruding horizontally from the centers of the pentagrams.

In white-fronted gown with lemon yellow arms and saffron hood, Issak Kidwell skips into ear-shot humming Dvorak's *Humoresque*.

——Some of them look like bees, Martin Fugat says. Others look like spiders.

——But none have nectar, Taft Merryweather says. Christians in the Victorian era believed this mimicry was intended to scare away insects so the flowers could, chastely, pollinate themselves.

The humming stops.

——Is that the traditional purpose of these hideous habits? Issak Kidwell asks delineating the kelly green cord of knotted rope around his waste. To force *us* to self pollinate?

——That's not allowed either, Taft Merryweather says showing teeth ear to ear. Number twenty-three fifty-two in the updated *Catechism of the Catholic Church*.

²ABELIA

When Flowers and Rocks are close-knit side by side,—
Sorting one from the other is part of the Veil;
Unity preaches that Subjects have lied,
Objects are present but boundaries fail.
Pink petals and pebbles were zero and one,
Then zero and zero as outlines were quashed;
Subtract the one zero it left You with None,
Which opened the Water in which I am washed.
My visible self didn't see what I viewed,
It worshipped dividing and truly believed;
Now sober narcotics float beautifully through,—
As dodging this Frame is deception deceived.
    Self-imposed are the fragments that hang on the vine,
    While opposites suckle both sides of Your line.

39 ¹ABELIAN

In a lawn-chair placed on top of a picnic table, Taft Merryweather suns himself while observing a patch of daffodils in front of the planetarium.

After twenty minutes, Gordon Flannery arrives seduced by the scene. In a walking meditation he begins to orbit Taft, moving closer and closer, in oblong circles.

——What are you doing? Taft Merryweather asks after seven revolutions.

——Distorting time, Gordon Flannery says. The better question is what are *you* doing?

Taft Merryweather stands while catching the analogy.

——Warping space, Taft Merryweather says.

^{2}ABELIAN

Taft Merryweather and Dale Rutherford reading articles about the world of the small.

——Allahu akbar! Taft Merryweather shouts.

——Allahu *h-bar*, Dale Rutherford says, is more like it.

Somewhere, in the jungles of Borneo, a butterfly tunnels directly *through* the massive trunk of a tree.

——So Yahweh-Elohim is Planck's constant? Taft Merryweather asks.

——Maybe God is, Dale Rutherford says shrugging his shoulders and yawning.

^{3}ABELIAN

You scan Left and then Right like this world is a page,
Three spatial dimensions your eyes will define;
Frontward and Backward the distance you gauge,
Up is the risen and Down the decline.
The secret of Empty's no secret at all,
You wake up each morning to stare at Its smile;
Without four dimensions your photons would fall,
While Spirit still equaled the Sun in denial.

When simple wave packets in truth do not age,
Their motion of time is diverted to space;
Complete with no remnant of time in its cage,
Confusing your Fullness and Primeval Face.
    The range of a boson with mystical lore,
      Is not proof of God…
               or His mystical Core.

40 [1]ABENAKI

Of a Buddhist monk in Jerusalem, Abbot Ezra says, one reads that when he was pursued by a Christian zealot, knowing this to be on account of the virtue of his testicles for medicinal purposes and not being able to escape, he stopped realizing what the Christian called his "*manifest destiny*"; and in order to be at peace with his pursuer sawed off his testicles with the dull end of a knife and handed them to his enemy, which he called… a *Crusader*.

[2]ABENAKI

An integral totem with Riches to show,
Stacks up in a column that's also a Spine;
Turquoise is the skin of the People that sew,
With Christian Electric from Hindu design.
The air wraps around carved wood in their back,
Which is bone that is painted invisible blue;
From this side of Kashmir it's a Muslim attack,
But only from boundaries both of them drew.
The vertebrate Krishna embodied true love,
Beyond his thoracic and lumbar support;
This cervical shelter for Triune Above,
Enveloped the Maxim that Sufis purport.
    Evolve through the zones and This you will favor,

Borders disappear when You are your neighbor.

41 [1]ABERDEEN

——You're charming and an ornament of the earth, Taft Merryweather says flipping bread-crumbs to the koi floating near the surface.

——An ornament of the earth? Martin Fugat says. What, in the name of Allah, do you mean?

Taft Merryweather thinks.

——You radiate with an active equilibrium, Taft Merryweather responds. But it's more than the broadcast of a tangible object. The Kosmos seems to be your satellite; not just some palpable core helping to define the position of your system. I mean, well, you magnify nature. And nature magnifies you. Whether you're tangled in a braid of flowers and leaves, hanging with Hugo upside-down from a tree by the backs of your knees, or swimming against the waves in the ocean, everything in the universe seems to swirl in a calm poetic vortex around the center that is *you*.

Martin Fugat, blushing, re-enacts the tightening of a neck-tie.

——Pop quiz! Martin Fugat says, modestly changing the subject. *If the globe was a Yule Tide Conifer, where on that tree would your ornament hang?*

——You tell me, Taft Merryweather says. There's a profusion of places to choose from.

——Scotland then, Martin Fugat randomly says. That answer was free. New question: *If the body was a bulb suspended from a branch, could it know of a soul on the inside?*

——Depends, Taft Merryweather says.

——Depends? Martin Fugat says. On what?

——The century in which you're living, Taft Merryweather says. Pick one.

——The eighteenth, Martin Fugat says.

——Then absolutely not, Taft Merryweather says. You're quiz is a bundle of perceptions.

²ABERDEEN

——Imagination doesn't mask reality, Issak Kidwell says to Silas Paul.
——*Routine* does, Taft Merryweather says.

³ABERDEEN

——William James, Dale Rutherford says, at the University of Edinburgh.

⁴ABERDEEN

A bundle of matches was rained on in spring,
As Christians were mocked for pre-rational views;—
Absent was mind or a Science would sing,
Dismissing Impressions in all that we choose.
Most Protestants claimed that the world wasn't Real,
While scientists sang that our thoughts were all matter;
Berkeley killed objects Perceiving who feels,
So mind held intact until Hume broke the ladder.
This dead-end was conquered by Savages Noble,
Then Kant strolled along chanting Knowledge Innate;
He divided three Districts which made them more mobile,
So Regions were walking in fragmented gaits.
    Four Quadrants are fusion of Plato's three Bands,
    Linking morals and art…
                 with the movements of sand.

42 [1]ABERRANT

The discussing of *Quantum Psalter* at the Round Table.

——Three hundred b.c., Abbot Ezra says.

——The Septuagint, Taft Merryweather responds.

——Turkish, Silas Paul says.

——K-U-R-apostrophe-A-N, Abe Hendrik responds.

——Four hundred a.d., Issak Kidwell says.

——The Vulgate, Gordon Flannery responds.

——Italian, Dale Rutherford says.

——C-O-R-A-N-O, Simon Warner responds.

——Thirteen-eighty-two, Martin Fugat says.

——The Wycliffe, Abbot Ezra responds.

——German, Taft Merryweather says.

——K-O-R-A-N, Silas Paul responds.

——Fifteen-twenty-five, Abe Hendrik says.

——The Tyndale, Issak Kidwell responds.

——French, Gordon Flannery says.

——C-O-R-A-N, Dale Rutherford responds.

——Fifteen-thirty-seven, Simon Warner says.

——The Coverdale, Martin Fugat responds.

——American, Abbot Ezra says.

——Q-U-R-apostrophe-A-N, Taft Merryweather responds.

——Sixteen-eleven, Silas Paul says.

——The King James, Abe Hendrik responds.

[2]ABERRANT

——The Buddha quit Sanskrit, Taft Merryweather says, to teach in the vernacular of the people.

³ABERRANT

An Aramaic guide ran fingers down his chest,
Touching the Qur'an and the Gita at his belt;
He wore a white toga and small woolen vest,
With pockets of Proverbs and poems he dealt.
A slip from a pouch he grants to a Friend,
On it is written a phrase in his tongue;
"If Non-dual is present then Stages you tend,"
So translated States are the height of one's rung.—
A Lattice of world-views these Axes display,
The Inside and Outside of one you call I;
Interior channels confine their own way,
But third person Research exposes their lie.
 Green spiders enlightened a Web might obey,
 Until its Expansion sees tulips in May.

43 ¹ABERRATION

——They're the summit of first-tier consciousness, Abbot Ezra says. For them, *all* meaning is context dependent.

——And therefore arbitrary, Dale Rutherford says twirling a finger in his soup.

——Pathological hermeneutics, Taft Merryweather says. They make Hamlet the equivalent of a photon.

——And Napoleon's life the equivalent of Don Quixote's, Dale Rutherford jokes.

——Or a line from Baudelaire the same as an integer from Einstein, Abbot Ezra says.

——Write this down, Dale Rutherford says. Poetry is not science, history is not fiction.

——What Taft said is better, Abbot Ezra says.

——By all means, Dale Rutherford says nodding to Taft.

——Pluralism is not Integralism, Taft Merryweather says.

[2]ABERRATION

——The Dharma was not constructed by the Buddha, Taft Merryweather says.

——It was discovered by him, Abe Hendrik says. The Dharma has always *been*.

[3]ABERRATION

No psalm can be written to slander your Living,
This Object of breathing no words can adorn;
No tapestries woven can tarnish its Giving,
When giving Itself is the reason you're born.
I studied the journals of Spirit's elite,
And this was the lesson from each that I learned;
Exchanging of symbols was how we could meet,
But under these symbols was Something that turned.
Transmitting this message I offer to you,
Short phrases of heaven involving the Soul;
My kosmic inclusion is mystically new,
With moments of Lila transcending the Whole.
    When patterns are ancient they're closer to fact,
    I'm pointing to Now…
                    which is Dharma Intact.

44 [1]ABET

——*Muid ad-Din ibn al-Arabi*, Silas Paul says. Eleven sixty-five to twelve forty.

——Read it again, Simon Warner says.

Silas Paul clears his throat.

——Do not attach yourself to any particular creed exclusively, so that you may disbelieve all the rest; otherwise you will lose much good, nay, you will fail to recognize the real truth of the matter. God, the omnipresent and omnipotent, is not confined to any one creed, for, he says, "Wheresoever ye turn, there is the face of Allah." Everyone praises what he believes; his god is his own creature, and in praising it he praises himself. Consequently he blames the beliefs of others, which he would not do if he were just, but his dislike is based on ignorance.

Taft Merryweather points to the stack on his desk. The Qur'an, Marcel Proust, the Gita, and a biography of Samuel Beckett.

——To the point, Simon Warner says with conviction. And, for me, perfectly affectionate.

²ABET

Even jonquils were trustless in the Garden of You,
When Petals suppressed came alive with a frown;
Unconscious these Lions that broke from your zoo,
Until they resurfaced as Anger you drowned.
This Shadow of Darkness infected your Heart,
But from you it's hidden, this split of your mind;
You managed an Ego then sliced it apart,
Afraid of the evil unbounded you bind.—
Resentment of self shows up as Mirage,
When emotions are dangled from Nouns in their wake;
The result of this fracture is motionless Hajj,
With you as the Pilgrim projecting your break.
   An umbra of silence will taint any Vision,
   Then rage in your garden…

              from lack of precision.

45 ¹ABEYANCE

Two letters were presented today, our last in Oporto. The first, from Prince Henry, included a spiel about Saint Ambrose's *De Noe et Arca*, discussing the history of the ship and rainbow as satisfactory symbols for the Christian Church. Rainbows, connected with the ark, for Ambrose and writers of his day symbolized *"the power to preserve all things and ensure their rebirth."* Henry's disregard for "the infidel" is notorious. By "the power to preserve all things," Henry, of course, means *all things Christian.* Little does he know that rainbows are also common symbols for the highest spiritual states of Muslims, Hindus, and Buddhists.

Carlo Cipriani and Marcel Fouquet have begun working on the *Psalter* by attempting a new form of sonnet. Copied below is part three of a trilogy re-telling the evolution of Abrahamic religion.

²ABEYANCE

With slippery tongues soft-smothered in wine,
I saw Muhammad kneel to a flower;
But these were not kisses of soft Compline,
Prophet to prophet un-masked in the hour.
These were the kisses with lips that converge,
Exploration granting exploration;
Tongue to tongue with philosophies that merge,
Crescent to Cross in obscure formation.
Jesus was the flower, his petals stiff,
Kneeling to the knelt, knelt to the kneeling;
Island to Island, with erotic drift,
Fingers in the place of magic feeling.
So Crescent and Cross made love without ties—
And spewing from both: *a star with twin sides.*

from the journals of Giovanni Landino, August 17, 1454.

46 [1]ABEYANT

———Although their claim is infinite, Dale Rutherford says, let's treat the problem as a finite set.

———So forget aleph-null and simplify, Gordon Flannery says.

Using red chalk, Dale Rutherford draws braces around a triumvirate of city-names.

———What's the cardinality? Gordon Flannery asks Taft.

———Three, Taft Merryweather says. Avignon, Rome, and Pisa.

[2]ABEYANT

Later that evening at the refectory.

———A real-life trinity, Abe Hendrik says behind his dinner roll. And settled at the Council of Constance.

———Turned three into one, Issak Kidwell says gulping wine.

———A new *scutum fidei*, Abbot Ezra says between bites of ambrosia. With Martin the fifth as the center node!

[3]ABEYANT

A Numen with reed pipe played notes in my ear,
Mathematics and jazz in a chasm of Love;
Dancing inaudibly Godhead was near,
Devouring the schism of Me from above.
I tip-toed in silence through Waves of Degree,
The silence was lovely like choc'late and art;
An orchestra joined adding silence to We,
Transcending this silence of You in my heart.
From nowhere to Nowhere I found where I am,
Beyond this bright silence was Stillness and Faith;
Saint John of the Cross is now One with the Lamb,

Which doubles my body as God and his Waif.
>This music's a sutra or transient thread,
>Thus I'm alive…

>>and impossibly Dead.

47 [1]ABHOR

——In Canto twenty-eight of *Inferno*, Taft Merryweather says, Dante places Muhammad in the eighth circle of hell.

——His body is filleted from beard to rectum, Abbot Ezra says. And his intestines are dangling and knocking against his knees.

[2]ABHOR

——During the Great Awakening, Simon Warner says, American Protestants interpreted the Seven Years War in eschatological terms. In light of this, November fifth became Pope's Day, an annual holiday celebrated by burning effigies of the Roman Pontiff.

[3]ABHOR

——Ethnocentric attacking ethnocentric, Martin Fugat says.

——Pitiful, Taft Merryweather says. But necessary.

[4]ABHOR

Vacationing Shiva to Eden is driven
To wither the Apples and poison the Pears;
For now he's assuming his Group is the given,
Exposing the Fear that mythology wears.
Although this is common with Gods at this level,
Shiva progressed and to Mecca was flown;

Transcending the Kaaba he out-grew the devil,
All Muslims were Human with Rights of their own.
A Relative Storm then swirled into action,
By limiting Apples the Pears could persist;
These Angels united in one massive faction,
Returning to Eden no truth could exist.
All three of these world-views are partial but true,
I'm embracing all three…

but transforming them too.

48 ¹ABHORRENCE

—Quote Voltaire, Taft Merryweather says to Silas Paul.

——If we believe in absurdities, Silas Paul says, we shall commit atrocities. Every sensible man, every honorable man, must hold the Christian sect in horror

——Quote Nietzsche, Taft Merryweather says.

——One does well, Silas Paul says, to put on gloves when reading the New Testament. The proximity of so much uncleanliness almost forces one to do so.

²ABHORRENCE

——In September of 2001, Issak Kidwell says, members who claimed to be from an Islamic fundamentalist organization hijacked four commercial airliners. Two of them were purposely crashed into skyscrapers of a major North American city.

³ABHORRENCE

——A lower form of world-centric awareness attacking the ethno-centric, Silas Paul says.

Taft Merryweather writes the word *hierarchy* in his notebook.
——And then vice-versa, Issak Kidwell says.

⁴ABHORRENCE

Remember atrocities done in the past?
Remember the Christians and Muslims who died?
Remember the Jews and the monks who were cast—
Early to graves in the name of a Lie?—
African slaughter and zealots will prove,
This Lie is still truth in their sphere of the Chain;
Crusades are a warning of why We should move—
Away from enshrining the Group that We feign.
Although it's a Station that all can transcend,
Some angels hit ceilings of Culture and Cult;
If violence is absent then Honor I send,
But still I must heed your ancestor's result.
  Medieval in Europe is third-world today,
  So God is not weeping…
                    when terrorists pray.

49 ¹ABHORRENT

——Alfred North Whitehead noticed it, Dale Rutherford says. He said the cosmos had been *reduced* to a dull affair, soundless, scentless, colorless; merely the hurrying of material, endlessly, meaninglessly.

——So did Michel Foucault, Gordon Flannery says. He said the totalitarian characteristics of an instrumental reason *objectifies* everything around it.

Gordon Flannery and Dale Rutherford ponder the off-spring of Democritus.

——*Itself included*, Dale Rutherford says.

[2]ABHORRENT

——The highest of first-tier world-centric awareness, Martin Fugat says, attacking the lower post-conventional mode.

——Typical, Taft Merryweather says. But necessary.

[3]ABHORRENT

Altitude couples with outlook to show,
The kosmic address in a Place with no center;
Without these two Points it's Abstraction you tow,
The World is pre-given and cancels your gender.
A tangible God is no longer required,
When concern for his proof has vanished to dust;
Referents are real in trans-rational Pyres,
But yearning for Other exhibits your lust.
I focused on candles unbroken for hours,
Then shifted this locus to Krishna and Christ;
Exemplars are learning that doctors will cower,
When Doctors of Soul remove God from their vice.
    How does one catch these invisible sparrows?
    They pair the internal…

                    with external arrows.

50 [1]ABIB

Skywriting in an air-craft a mile above the shore-lines of Ambrojjio, Abe Hendrik sings as his plane, tacking vertically with nimble precision, swoops right and dips around emitting a side-ways fog-colored parabola.

——I didn't know Abe was a pilot, Taft Merryweather says squinting archaically into an abyss that was once called The Heavens.

——Because he's not, Simon Warner says. Brother Abe is just along for the ride.

——As we all are, Abbot Ezra says. None of us are pilots. The most we can be is *co-pilot*.

Abe Hendrik, gliding opposite gravity at a semi-steep grade, upon reaching his pinnacle, loops half the symbol for infinity then downwardly floats mirroring the brush-stroke of his initial line. After pausing to re-adjust, he darts with his jet through a transient pyramid; leaving a shelf of white smoke in the process.

——Then who's flying? Taft Merryweather says watching Hugo trace the dancing sky-born shadow with his arms out-stretched like *Vitruvian Man*.

——The freckled Cessna in sneakers *right in front of you*, Simon Warner says. Terrestrially known as Hugo Gustafson.

Duplicating the in-flight maneuvers used to create the opening exercise, Abe Hendrik adds a descending slanted crutch to the joint of the bar and parabola.

——P-A-R!, P-A-R!, Hugo Gustafson chants oblivious to his surroundings.

A vapor-trail, the shape of a tea-cup handle, steadily appears on the light-blue canvas of a cloudless sky.

——No really, Taft Merryweather says. Who's flying the plane?

——*I am*, Simon Warner says giving Taft an ancient glare.

——And so are you, Abbot Ezra says to Taft grabbing his hand and squeezing.

The letter E now achieved, Abe Hendrik slivers from the left, bends upward, angles back, then curves a rounded surface until his partner achieves completion.

——P-A-R-D-E-S! Hugo Gustafson shouts into the breeze.

——Pardes, Simon Warner says pronouncing it for Hugo.

In the distance, an exclamation point emerges into view.

——Paradise, Taft Merryweather says.

——Yes, Abbot Ezra says. *Paradise*.

²ABIB

Paradise is sleeping with jungles and stars,
It feels with two hands and a mind like your own;
It dives into Shadows and fuses with Scars,
Then centers the axis of Shadow to Bone.
These Luminous Pipers are silent but Loud,
Their song is concrete yet transparent to sight;
Content with non-dual even One is a crowd,
Yet structures are Perfect Eternal Delight.
This Portal is present and never will veer,
It's moving with you as you're reading this page;
No angels are winking or Rational jeers,
Just Beautiful Sanity living with change.
   Nirvana is seeping through shapes made of ink,
   These Statues were dead...
                     but then suddenly blink.

BOOK TWO

GOD'S CARNIVAL, GOD'S ROCKS

51 ¹ABIDANCE

The Child Rabbinical Orchid in the Muslim Tao of Christ grips the fluttering sash of his mother's dress, being lead for the countless numbered time through an artfully trimmed gap in an ample spread of saw-grass which he knows will eventually dissolve as the sand thickens and then erupt at an angle into a jagged cliff which offers a natural stair-case, jutting in peaceful increments, allowing for an uneventful leisurely climb to his heavenly promontory over-looking the ocean. As he files along, he reflects on how his personages have matured over the years. At seven, in his first months at Rainbow Abbey, he was a ubiquitous Spirit; a mid-summer Ariel enchanting every aspect of his private island, from the fluff on the dandelions to the minarets and stained-glass windows that seemed to bring God within range of his finger-tips. Later, after praying with Simon Warner, he solidified into an Occidental explorer of the Great Silk Road. With his magnifying glass and an internal calumet sophisticated beyond the appearance of his physical make-up, Hugo Gustafson began to comb the land-scape of Ambrojjio and to absorb the ideas of various Quantums into his impressionable but magnetic mind. It was during this time that he wrote his first poem about Europe being a peninsula of Asia. And now, at age eleven, as he scales this familiar crag with his mother, he pretends to be a traveling mendicant, a Dominican or Friars Minor or maybe even a Theravadan bhikku, intent on sharing his blessings with the fur and feathers he sees frolicking in trees and on the carnival of the ground which includes all life on the rock upon which he stands.

——Father Simon said it, Hugo Gustafson says. A little closer to the sun and the oceans would vaporize.

Hugo fails to comprehend a little farther and the oceans would freeze.

——Is this what frightens you? Hugo's mother asks.

——Nothing is frightening, Hugo says sincerely. *I just wonder why everything has turned out so Perfect.*

²ABIDANCE

——Born in the darkness of interstellar space some 4.6 billion years ago, our solar system emerged from a contracting molecular cloud of dust and gas. When the core of this cloud became dense enough, gravity triggered the collapse of its inner layers causing matter to fall inward for perhaps a million years as internal heat, trapped by the gases, fired up a protosun and ignited thermonuclear reactions. Rotation drew the material into a swirling nebular disk. Its hot innermost constituents drifted farther inward, enlarging the protosun until a powerful gaseous outflow from the solar inferno blasted away the infalling material, unveiling our newborn sun in all its brilliance. The cooler, more distant portions of the nebula contained the raw material of a planetary system.

Dale Rutherford's presentation kindles Abe Hendrik into cautionary day-dreams of the *Cosmic* Big-Top.

——Within its self-contained universe of rings, Abe Hendrik says, this *Cosmic* Circus offers metaphysical entertainment. It showcases the interconnectedness of the human and the animal and the non-human. Then it hypnotizes its spectators, forcing them to believe that its performers have the potential to transfigure physical laws when in essence the performers *are those physical laws*, or at least have the potential to *become* them.

——Paging Abe Hendrik, Abbot Ezra says to his monks in a ruckus of guffawing and knee-slapping laughter.

——*Kosmic* with a K, Abe Hendrik says still lost to the world. Not *Cosmic*.

³ABIDANCE

Already the legendary poet of his home-town in the Punjabi region of northern India; and with an inflating unsolicited cult-like following from both The Slade and the Ecole des Beaux-Arts; the autodidactic Silas Paul, lover of ashrams, ideograms, and the insights of religious collage, steadily continues to chisel and paint his limestone combinations of poetry and sculpture.

——So the figure of the Hindu-Sufi harlequin is almost ready, Taft Merryweather says parting a curtain of glass beads dividing Silas Paul's studio from the corridor.

——Call it what you will, Silas Paul says tucking a mallet into the holster of his over-alls. For me, it's a color-coded ascending second-tier *Sikh keshdhari granthi.*

Taft rubs his hand along the smoothness of the statue.

——The inscription on the pedestal, Silas Paul says, will be adapted from the *Guru Granth Sahib*. It goes something like this:

I collected the spectrum of molasses such that it turned my body into firewood.

> Then wine trickled from the roof of the house of pleasure
> > by means of the furnace of my heart.
> Describe him as intoxicated with the wine of divine love
> Who drinketh the sweetness of our planet's name
> > and meditateth on divine knowledge.
> Since the server of the wine of divine love met me
> > and gave it to me,
> My days and nights are passing away intoxicated
> > with the comedy of angels.
> Their dust is mingled with the circus of my laughter.
> Clown-Hindu! Clown-Muslim! Clown-Christian! Clown-Jew!
> Let's tease ourselves with the silence of our painted faces.

Let's take deep breaths together as we swallow the moon!

52 ¹ABIDE

——If you bring forth what is within you, Abbot Ezra says, what you bring forth will save you. If you do not bring forth what is within you, what you do not bring forth will destroy you.

——That's Yeshua from the Gospel of Thomas, Issak Kidwell says wrapping his Rosary beads around the base of his ring finger. Discovered at Nag Hammadi in a mountain honey-combed with hundreds of Egyptian caves.

——For orthodox Christians, Martin Fugat says while crossing himself, the transformational power of this Jewish bodhisattva sits trapped in their brains like a breathing fossil.

——Because consciousness is stratified, Abbot Ezra says. Like layers of the Earth. Yeshua's message is waiting to be *excavated*.

——So we Quantum Catholics need to encourage a generation of spiritual archaeologists, Issak Kidwell says.

——And that would be the simple part, Martin Fugat says. After excavation comes *integration*. The artifacts from each level must be recognized and then embraced.

——And after integration comes *activation*, Abbot Ezra says. This lack of knowledge leaves mythical religion stuck on an unrevolving Ferris Wheel.

——The leaders of these institutions, Issak Kidwell says, must be made to realize that this Wheel has cogs for a purpose. Their responsibility is not to bring the gears before and after to a grinding halt. Their vocation is the transference of energy to the intermeshing gear in waiting.

——This applies to Muslims, Martin Fugat says, Buddhists, Hindus, Sikhs, and Jews until infinity.

——Excavate, integrate, activate, Abbot Ezra says. This is the Quantum *Aggiornamento*.

²ABIDE

——So far as the history of European sculpture is concerned, Silas Paul says to Gordon Flannery, by far the most important development was the discovery, probably in fifth century axial Greece, of a technique that enabled a sculptor to carve in stone an accurate replica of a human model made of clay, plaster, or some other easily manipulated substance. The model was marked at four extremities with 'points' and then the distances between them and a plumb line or wooden structure were measured so that holes of equivalent depth could be drilled into a marble block at the corresponding points or levels. The material between these holes was then chiseled away to reveal a rough version of the human model.

——Starting from the periphery of the cross-hairs and moving inward, Gordon Flannery says relating Silas Paul's speech to philosophy. The further we evolve as humans, the smaller the amount of stone that will need to be removed. This is physics, biology, psychology, theology; all in a single frame-work.

53 ABIGAIL

In 1535 Saint Teresa neglected the wishes of her family, running away to become a Carmelite nun at the Convent of the Incarnation at Avila. Spending long periods of her life under the influence of both Dominicans and Jesuits, it was an anonymous letter from Peter of Alcantara that inspired a return to her devotional book, *Abecedario Espiritual* (The Spiritual Alphabet), and informed her of an assemblage of monk-poets hard at work on a more complicated but similar venture at a mystical monastery somewhere nearby on an island in the North Atlantic. Learning of the creative freedoms present at Rainbow Abbey but being plagued by ill health herself, Saint Teresa arranged a voyage to Ambrojjio for three of her closest confidants at Avila. These three nuns studied at Rainbow Abbey for ten solid years before setting sail to establish their own residence in Rome which today is less than a mile from St. Peter's square in Vatican City.

——We at Rainbow Abbey work closely with our sisters at Quantum Convent, Abbot Ezra says. The *Psalter* is most definitely matropater and masculofeminine. Or in other words: *androgynous*.

54 ¹ABILITY

It's been less than a year since our arrival at the Isle of Man and already we are forced to transition with the election of a new Pope. Our non-local affiliation with the Holy See leaves the future of our psalm writing uncertain. Giovanni Landino, our leader selected by Pope Nicholas, is immediately writing to the current Pontiff in regards to the potential fruitfulness of Rainbow Abbey's combination of work, prayer, and study. Our time here is off to as good a start as could be expected. Along the numerous fresh-water streams, the country-side is now speckled with dozens of hermitages and the beginnings of our first cathedral. A cellar has been completed to house the thousands of manuscripts we brought from the main-land and the hundreds of volumes which have already arrived with fresh shipments of provisions from Portugal. My reading and contemplation of celebrated writers from numerous spiritual traditions has opened a vast clean space of awareness. For me, there's a delicate elegance waiting to emerge if people would awaken to a thoughtfulness of co-owning this exhilarating Region Without Regions. Promotion, such as this, belongs in the *Psalter*. For example:

Gifted Angels romp and sing-
Oblivious of My sacred cathedral in
Denmark.
Somewhere in the West, a Dazzling Gnome
Contemplates the slaughter of Plato's
Academy.—
Raptured Angels
Nod and flex-

Intuiting My cathedral and the integral

Values of Denmark.

Alive in the East, a Dazzling Gnome

Liberates the daughter of Plato's Academy.—

Genuine Angels walk and fly-

Operating on My sacred cathedral in

Denmark.

Somewhere in the North, a Dazzling Gnome

Reiterates the

Oriental

Comfort of Plato's Academy.—

Knitting Rainbows in the

South, this Danish Gnome awakens to Denmark.

from the journals of Francesco Mola, July 9, 1455

[2]ABILITY

——In Dr. C.H. Wu's Chinese translation of the New Testament, Abbot Ezra says, he opens the Gospel of John in the following way: *"In the beginning was the Tao."*

55 [1]AB INITIO

——The New Testament, Martin Fugat says. John chapter three, verses five through eight.

Truly I tell you,
no one can enter the kingdom of God
without being born of water and Spirit.
What is born of human nature is human;
what is born of the Spirit is spirit.

Do not be surprised when I say:
You must be born anew.
The breath of the wind blows where it pleases.
You can hear its sound,
but you cannot tell where it comes from or where it goes.
So it is with everyone who is born of the Spirit.

——With reference to "being born of water and Spirit," Abe Hendrik says, the average Quantum might think of Genesis I:I and the time when "darkness was upon the face of the deep, and God's Spirit breathed over the face of the waters." It is an under-noticed fact that in Genesis God does not create darkness but contains it. After creating light, "God *separated* the light from the darkness. God called the light Day, and the darkness he called Night. And there was evening, and there was morning, the first day". Day, which God had created, is a space cleared within darkness, which he did not create. Time begins when light begins, occupying the same cleared space in the primeval darkness, which itself is timeless. "And God said: 'Let there be lights in the firmament of the heavens to separate the day from the night; *and let them be for signs and for seasons and for days and for years*'". As light is a space cleared within darkness, so time is a space cleared within eternity by God's chronometers, the sun, *the moon*, and the stars. As for the waters, once again God does not create them but only contains or restrains them, opening dry land as an ordered space within the chaos of the waters: "Let the waters under the heavens be gathered together into one place, and let the dry land appear". Night and ocean as mankind knows them are the remains of the uncreated chaos of darkness and water that God dammed up to make the world.

[2]AB INITIO

——A 'Z' is a dismantled 'A', Hugo Gustafson says skipping rocks across the lens of a pond. Re-arranged into what you call the Ground

Unconscious.

——I suppose that's correct, Simon Warner says snapping into the flesh of an apple. Your 'A' is my 'Spirit.' And Spirit is always present as the cycle of this Serious Comedy continues to advance. In your terms I would say that Ground Unconscious is the 'Z' that progressively forgot it was the 'A'.

Hugo Gustafson hurls a flat stone into the warmth of the air which boomerangs and returns to its sender.

——So 'A' injects 'Z' with a Kosmos of potential, Hugo Gustafson says holding out his palm for a sliver of fruit. But 'Z' can only bloom by waking up to the 'A' that is already in existence.

——That's close, Simon Warner says contemplating evolution.

——How else would you phrase it? Hugo Gustafson asks.

——The 'A' is not only *in* existence, Simon Warner answers Hugo. Spirit *is* existence. Existence as an unblemished entirety.

[3]AB INITIO

The flexing cross-hairs named Equator and Prime Meridian.

——Ambrojjio's latitude is thirty-five degrees North, Dale Rutherford says.

——Ambrojjio's longitude is forty-five degrees West, Gordon Flannery says.

56 ABIOGENESIS

Mossy rocks and clear riffles in a timid synchronicity with the minnows' breathing. A catalogue of jonquils in a fissure parallel with the creek. One of those afternoons when Taft Merryweather is openly sly with the Demiurge. He blatantly relaxes while dreaming of raspberry truffles and Tantric episodes of himself with the Virgin Mary. Transcending morality, in theory, is a delightful frame-work. Hugs for everyone, kosmically speaking. And more than hugs for most.

——In our time Venus is confused and Apollo sound asleep, Ezra Davenport says.

But Taft doesn't hear him. Taft Merryweather is on his knees absorbed by the scene. He stares through his reflection and is witness to the dozens of minnows beneath the surface. Their pulsating gills are in unison like an orchestra of biological accordions. Taft melts into the water glancing up from the stream and is arrested by the jonquils in a turquoise love-knot with an indigo breeze. The universe turns violet with a texture infested with the sweetness of cinnamon and butterscotch. *The jonquils are dancing... We are dancing... I am dancing... Dancing...*

——Cosmic Microwave Background Radiation, Abbot Ezra says writing the word *isotropic* on a chalk-board.

Taft rises from his desk and faces the sangha.

——Involution-Evolution, Taft Merryweather says.

57 ABIOGENIC

On an arid Monday morning with a *crescent* moon still visible in the sky, Silas Paul unveils his latest sculpture to a gathering crowd outside the planetarium. He titles it, "The Five K's: Keshdhari Khadija's Kundalini Kabalistic Kerygma."

——All of this is Brahman, Silas Paul says designing an imaginary heart using both his hands for bilateral symmetry. This Truth of things that has to emerge out of the phenomenal world's contradictions is declared to be an infinite Bliss and self-conscious Existence, the same everywhere, in all things, in all times beyond Time, and aware of itself behind all these phenomena by whose intensest vibrations of activity or by whose largest totality it can never be entirely expressed or in any way limited; for it is self-existent and does not depend for its being upon its manifestations. They represent it, but do not exhaust it; point to it, but do not reveal it. It is revealed only to itself within their forms. The conscious existence involved in the form comes, as it evolves, to know itself by intuition, by self-vision, by self-experience. It becomes itself in the world by knowing itself; it knows itself by becoming itself.

The crowd applauds. Martin Fugat releases a dove while Hugo Gustafson performs a cartwheel for the Mass to observe.

——Hurray for the Sufi harlequin and Sri Aurobindo! Taft Merryweather shouts.

Silas Paul knowingly rolls his eyes.

——*Tat tvam asi*, Silas Paul says acknowledging Hugo and smiling at Martin Fugat.

——Wonderful, isn't it? Martin Fugat says to Taft. Let's take deep breaths together as we swallow the moon.

58 ABIOLOGICAL

——Natal charts and personal transits, Hugo Gustafson says handing Silas Paul a book about astrology.

——You called this informative? Silas Paul asks with a sense of hesitation.

——Definitely, Hugo Gustafson says assured of his genius. According to tradition, there are ten planetary archetypes: Sun, Moon, Mercury, Venus, Mars, Jupiter, Saturn, Uranus, Neptune, and Pluto.

Silas Paul un-tethers a trio of balloons from Hugo Gustafson's wrist.

——*Elevationism*, Taft Merryweather chimes from the neighboring desk.

——What's that? Hugo Gustafson asks.

——Let me guess, Silas Paul says intercepting Taft's train of thought. You read about the Sun being a symbol for the Hero in all its forms. It illuminates the world as a nuclear furnace and a beacon of ontology.

Hugo Gustafson squirms in his seat.

——How'd you know? Hugo Gustafson asks.

——It's a common fallacy nowadays, Silas Paul says. You're confusing authentic spirituality with a more primitive, pre-rational form of cognizance.

——Give this to Father Simon, Taft Merryweather says conferring a bag of cotton-candy upon Hugo. Tell him Taft said to teach you the differences between *pre* and *trans* levels of consciousness.

59 [1]ABIOTIC

——Perhaps, Dale Rutherford says, the most widely accepted theory of cell aging is the *genetic theory*, which suggests that cessation of mitosis and cell aging are programmed into our genes. One interesting notion here is that a *telomere clock* determines the number of times a cell can divide. Telomeres are strings of nucleotides that cap the end of chromosomes, protecting them from fraying or fusing with other chromosomes. In human telomeres, the base sequence TTAGGG is repeated a thousand times or more. Though the telomeres carry no genes, they appear to be vital for chromosomal survival, because each time DNA is replicated, fifty to one hundred of the end nucleotides are lost and the telomeres get a bit shorter. When telomeres reach a certain minimum length, the stop-division signal is given. The idea that cell longevity depends on telomere integrity is supported by the 1994 discovery of *telomerase*, an enzyme that protects telomeres from degrading. Pegged as the "immortality enzyme," telomerase is almost universally found in cancer cells, but not in other cell types.

[2]ABIOTIC

Mounting steps to the Quantum *Stupa*.

——Birth is the condition of having no past, Taft Merryweather says.

——Death is the condition of having no future, Abe Hendrik replies.

The dome and the monoliths glide into view.

——Therefore Time is a dimension, Silas Paul says.

³ABIOTIC

Glorious Maimonides, Angel
Of Judaism,
During celebration of Parinirvana
Spattered a dozen Christian beds of
Calendula with
Aromatic mirth. He emphasized that
Returning to Christ was
Nothing but an
Individual
V*alidation* of the
Astral qualities of
Lotus Sutra
Grounded in a garden
Of necessary
Duhkha or
Suffering.
Respecting the partial nature
Of this truth and
Care, We as the
Kosmos
Salute him.

60 ¹ABJECT

——*Cleave* is a double entendre, Silas Paul says to Issak Kidwell. Its definition means *both* to split and to adhere.

——Reminds me of God's Polish polymath, Gordon Flannery says. Copernicus split the earth from the center of the universe and coerced it to adhere to the menu of *wanderers* drifting around the sun.

——*Heliocentric*, Hugo Gustafson says meandering through a gate to

The Hall of Vertebrates hand in hand with Silas Paul.

——Well done! Issak Kidwell says to Hugo combining it with a look of endorsement. You seem to be growing more intelligent by the second.

——Thank you much, Hugo Gustafson responds debonairly. *Father Simon says this theory made us bi-peds for the very first time.*

——Never thought of it that way, Issak Kidwell says offering the free end of a twig shaped like a wish-bone to Gordon Flannery.

——Nor I, Gordon Flannery admits snapping the wish-bone in two.

Hugo Gustafson steals the larger half from Issak, quickly composing an invocation.

——But now that I am, Silas Paul says, Brother Simon decidedly has a point.

²ABJECT

——The thistle is a redwood in her galloping microcosm, Martin Fugat says.

——And this proved common knowledge, Abe Hendrik says, for those who knew it.

61 ¹ABJECTION

——It happened while on a retreat to Mount Hira, Abbot Ezra says. On the seventeenth night of Ramadan.

——It's also known as the Mountain of Light, Silas Paul interjects. *Jabal al-Nour* in Arabic.

——But after this initial revelation, Abbot Ezra says, there was an extended hiatus. Muhammad tormented himself with thoughts of causing God displeasure.

——However, Silas Paul says, the second revelation eventually arrived via the auspices of the Sufi-Benedictine pandit, Gabriel. It's now Surah ninety-three in the Recitation called "The Early Hours of Morning Witness."

In the Name of Allah-Yeshua-Elohim, The Compassionate, The Confusing

"I" Call To Witness
    the early hours of morning,
And the night when the dark and still are continuous...
The Witness can neither leave you
    nor despise you.
What is to come is better for you
    than what has gone before;
For the Witness knows not the difference.
Did it not find you an orphan
    and take care of you?
Did it not find you perplexed,
    and show you the way?
Did it not find you poor
    and enrich you?
So do not oppress the orphan,
And do not drive the beggar away:
For you _are_ the orphan,
And so are you the beggar.
Thus recount the favors of your vanished Lord.

——After hearing that, Abbot Ezra says, I think Yeshua may have been a Muslim mystic.

——I agree, Silas Paul says. It's like the at-onement in the Garden of Gethsemani.

²ABJECTION

——Ahmad ibn Majid's first poem appeared in 1462, Martin Fugat says. It's title was _Hawiya_.

62 ABJURATION

Communal breakfast at the dining hall.

——See Muhammad, slay Muhammad! Taft Merryweather spontaneously shouts into Silas Paul's ear pouring milk over his cereal.

The Quantums at the table snicker in amusement.

——Is that Muslim Zen? Silas Paul asks facetiously.

——What's Zen? Taft Merryweather replies. Every copy of the Qur'an is ashes.

——I understand that, Silas Paul says with gusto. You're pointing to the fact that *imitation is slavery*.

——Fact? Taft Merryweather asks bewildered. Who *are* you?

Taft Merryweather grabs his copy of the Koran and deposits it into Silas Paul's lap.

——All modes of life need independence to grow, Silas Paul says. A *living* truth can never be fixed into a formula, creed, or catechism.

——See Yeshua, murder Yeshua! Taft Merryweather shouts.

——That's the beauty of your updating trans-Benedictine monastic law, Silas Paul says to Taft. It becomes available to us only as we give ourselves to it.

Taft Merryweather snatches his Coran from Silas Paul's lap.

——Freedom is neither compulsive nor conforming, Silas Paul says. Living *creatively* goes beyond formality.

Silas Paul pushes Taft's bundle of literature causing it to slam onto the floor.

——See the Buddha, kill the Buddha! Taft Merryweather shouts.

63 ¹ABJURE

Star-gazing in the Northern Hemisphere.

——Quantum Monday, Martin Fugat says.

——Moon, Gordon Flannery responds.

——*Shrove Tuesday*, Martin Fugat says.

——Mars, Gordon Flannery responds.

——Ash Wednesday, Martin Fugat says.

——Mercury, Gordon Flannery responds.

——Maundy Thursday, Martin Fugat says.

——Jupiter, Gordon Flannery responds.

——Good Friday, Martin Fugat says.

——Venus, Gordon Flannery responds.

——Holy Saturday, Martin Fugat says.

——Saturn, Gordon Flannery responds.

——Easter Sunday, Martin Fugat says.

——*Earth*, Gordon Flannery responds.

²ABJURE

——The shape of Earth, Dale Rutherford says, is *oblate* spheroid.

64 ABLATE

With red cinders and red death, the Quantum imagination becomes a super-natural hoedown. Then suddenly the carved message in the maple tree renders like an Indian Genesis.

——In the beginning, Silas Paul says, there was a Baltic soup in a massive kettle, the ingredients being an egg with an extra rib, a bowl of seeds, a block of salt, and many gallons of water.

——This was hung from the sculpted cross-bar, Taft Merryweather says, over the densely packed fire and placed behind the prison with no way out, and this behind the infinite shroud.

——The recipe was simmered on the slowest heat, Dale Rutherford says, blending the oceans gradually; the yolk and rib forming the tribe of primitive white protocols, the seeds swelling into bundles of clean top-soil.

——Time was in the future, Abe Hendrik says. But on the stage it was one coincidental barn dance after another.

——Followed by a community bar-hop, Abbot Ezra says. Where the suds rose to the brim and over the brim.

——Pushing a cat-fish into the flames, Issak Kidwell says.

——And this sparked the kosmic dynamite, Simon Warner says.

——Which ultimately proved the world.

65 [1]ABLATION

Existing in the boundaries of Silas Paul's studio, Simon Warner and Hugo Gustafson sluggishly examine statues in the sculptor's display case.

——A fallacious and impoverished self-image is called the *Persona*, Simon Warner says to Hugo Gustafson.

Hugo thinks back to his lessons for the day.

——Isn't that from the Latin for *mask*? Hugo Gustafson asks.

——It is, Simon Warner says. But let's take this a bit further. Have you ever heard of the *Shadow*?

——I haven't, Hugo Gustafson says zeroing in on a particular work of art.

——The Shadow, Simon Warner says, is the disowned, alienated, and projected facets of the Ego which appear to be arriving from the external world.

Hugo Gustafson sleepily nods, more interested in the sculpture than in the conversation.

——Those are my replicas of the *Venus de Milo*, Silas Paul says entering the room through a barrier of glass beads. She's symbolic for me because she has no arms to embrace what she truly adores.

——Did you amputate them? Hugo Gustafson asks employing his middle and index fingers to make a motion like clipping scissors.

——*Venus* willingly did it to herself, Simon Warner interrupts returning to his topic of psychology. She probably has what neurologists identify as *phantom limbs*.

——So she's kind of like the Shadow, Hugo Gustafson says unaware he had grasped Simon's teaching. Her extremities aren't there. But her mind is projecting them as being so.

²ABLATION

——The Taj Mahal, Issak Kidwell says, is India's noble tribute to the grace of Indian womanhood.

——The Venus de Milo of the East, Silas Paul says.

66 ABLATIVE

——The very finest particles of rock carried by melt-water streams, Abe Hendrik says, are smaller than sand grains and sometimes called *rock flour*. They are produced by the scouring action of ice on under-lying bedrock, and are so minute they remain suspended for very long periods of time which gives glacial lakes their characteristic *turquoise* color. The scraping and scratching and polishing that produces rock flour leaves very distinctive telltale marks on under-lying bedrock. But it's not the ice itself that does the grinding. Ice at temperatures well below freezing is still too soft to gouge out scratches in solid rock.

——It was actually the rock debris, Gordon Flannery says, carried by the ice that produced these scratches. Rocks and pebbles embedded in the ice were being dragged across the under-lying surface. These glaciers were like gigantic sheets of sandpaper smoothing out the rocks beneath. When scientists were eventually able to map the movement of ice within glaciers, they discovered that the base of a glacier is continually renewed with ice from above, complete with its embedded grit. This natural sandpaper, therefore, *is constantly being refreshed.*

Silas Paul moves his lips closer to Issak Kidwell's ear.

——*Lila*, Silas Paul says to Issak.

67 [1]ABLATIVE ABSOLUTE

Dale Rutherford speaks Latin for the desired effect:

——*Cuius regio, eius religio*, Dale Rutherford says.

But Ezra demands that Rutherford's obscurity will only ossify convictions. The dualistic response will be:

——Faith Island is more than a tactic, Ezra Davenport says. It's the construction by God of a ponderable masterpiece.

Issak intercedes:

——*My God is below the waste, believe it*! Issak Kidwell shouts.

The same God is above the ankles and above the knees.

Taft Merryweather responds from the water-fountain:

——*Hey Issak! We monotheistics should band together, ha*!

Ezra shakes his head emphatically and Gordon Flannery chuckles at the lack of evolution.

[2]ABLATIVE ABSOLUTE

Across the bottom of the page of his self-painted mandala, Hugo Gustafson pens in his fanciest calligraphy:

"*Ex divina pulchritudine esse omnium derivatur.*"

68 ABLAUT

The intuition of Triple Vision.

——Without death, resurrection is impossible, Martin Fugat says. In *The Acts of the Apostles*, Yeshua woke up for forty days then ascended in a cloud from a peak on Mount Olivet near the village of Bethany.

——*Fly*! Silas Paul exclaims.

——The Prophet Muhammad, Abe Hendrik says, had a similar experience. When he was making his Nocturnal Journey from Arabia to the Temple Mount in Jerusalem, he was greeted by Yeshua, Moses, Abraham and a slew of other prophets before climbing a ladder through the Seven Heavens which lead him directly to the Divine Sphere.

——*Flew*! Silas Paul exclaims.

——Second Kings, chapter two, verses nine through twelve, Taft Merryweather says. The Original Testament claims Elijah was carried to heaven in a whirl-wind.

——*Homo Religiosis*, Abbot Ezra says.

Taft Merryweather optimistically predicts an avalanche of love.

——*Flown*! Silas Paul exclaims.

69 ¹ABLAZE

Seated around the camp-fire, Abbot Ezra Davenport converses with an organization of Jewish retreatants.

——The ceremony of the *sama*, Abbot Ezra says, is conducted in a very specific way. The dancers enter wearing white robes, symbols of the shroud, enveloped in ample black coats, representing the tomb, and coiffed with high felt hats, images of the tombstone. The sheikh, who represents the intermediary between the heavens and the earth, enters last. He salutes the dervishes and they return the gesture. He then sits in front of the red carpet whose shade evokes the color of the setting sun. The singer celebrates the praises of the Prophet *a capella* with a text written by Rumi and music by the great Turkish composer Itri. After this, the flutist begins improvising while the dervishes advance slowly and turn three times around the dance floor. The three rounds are symbolic of the three stages that take one nearer to God: the path of science, the path of vision and the path leading to the union with God.

Abbot Ezra lights a stick of incense.

——At the end of the third turn the sheikh takes his place on the carpet. The dervishes let their black coats fall, springing out of them wearing white as if liberated from their earthly envelope for a second birth. They ask the sheikh for permission to dance and then start whirling slowly, spreading their arms like wings, the right palm turned upward toward the sky to gather divine grace, and the left palm pointed downward to return it to the earth. This grace has crossed their hearts and has been warmed by their love. *The movement they perform around the floor represents the universal law, the planets turning around the sun and around their own center.* The drums evoke the trumpets of the last judgment. The circle of dancers is divided into two semi-circles, one represents the Arc of Descent, or the involution of Soul into matter; the other represents the Arc of Ascent, or the evolution of Soul toward God.

Abbot Ezra's guests prepare for the Quantum liturgy.

——The sheikh enters the dance at the fourth turn as the rhythm doubles in time, becoming very rapid. The sheikh turns at the center of the circle representing the sun and its rays. When he enters the dance the *ney* improvises again. This improvisation is the supreme moment of the achieved union. When the sheikh returns to his place, the *sama* is over and the singer recites the Qur'an; God's words answer the dervishes:

——*Anywhere you turn is the Hidden Face of Jesus*, Taft Merryweather says.

²ABLAZE

——Humans vibrate at forty-two octaves above middle C, Gordon Flannery whispers to Silas Paul.

In front of the congregation Dale Rutherford recites a portion of the *Fire Sermon*.

——*Spontaneous combustion*, Silas Paul responds.

3ABLAZE

Glorious al-Ghazali, Angel
Of Islam,
During the ascension of Isra Miraj

Sifted through pages of an English Qur'an

Composing mystical

Anecdotes for non-mystical

Rabbis who chose to

Neglect the

Incoherence of philosophy. These

Vicissitudes of

Aristotle's *updating*

Linger in the transcendental

Gymnasiums

Of

Diamond

Suras forever.

Respecting the partial nature

Of this truth and

Care, We as the

Kosmos

Salute him.

70 ¹ABLE

Simon Warner and Abe Hendrik composing a poem about Taft Merryweather.

——The strange delicious creeds of synthetic fruits have grown fat in the orchards of history.

——But for Taft Merryweather, Abe Hendrik says, *the questions remain*.

——So gingerly and lovingly, Simon Warner says, in a voice that would curve the fabric of the driest leaf, Taft Merryweather hums as he sinks his knees into an alter at the river's edge.

——Then he weeps as he prays for men who evolve into paranoid symposiums of sacred disaster.

——In his mind, Simon Warner says, every tear that drips from his eye is a hymn to bring peace to these men being stunned by embroidered gesture.

——And every sob is a prayer for their children being taught to magnify the past and to prepare for the future.

——*In this way*, Simon Warner says, *losing the eternal present has become a disease.*

——And it leaves us with a world that is filled with restless souls, who although at home, are ninety percent gypsy and only ten percent chrysalis.

——Sadly, Simon Warner says, the telling of our story is one that consists of violated bones, half-eaten cores, old books, curled worms, and other fetid emblems of human waste that pledge allegiance to their parents' graves.

——But aware of this or not, Abe Hendrik says, *the carnival of the land is a museum in our blood.*

——And the essence of hope, Simon Warner says, is knowing that prophets can flower from the innards of this chamber pot.

——So finally, Abe Hendrik says, while digging in the depths of the weirdest orchids of his religious mind, Taft Merryweather attempts to cultivate the *pulp* of every cloister.

——He fumbles his hairy shoulders, Simon Warner says, from under the straps of his small pack.

——He wades twelve steps into the sun-drenched river.

——He sighs, he grins, he rolls his eyes.

——*And then he blinks.*

²ABLE

——There's only one Christ, Martin Fugat says plucking a pear from its limb.

——And there's only one Prophet, Silas Paul responds nabbing a pear from the same branch.

——It's a matter of *potential*, Issak Kidwell says going for an apple instead.

——Which means there are infinite Buddhas, Taft Merryweather claims picking an apple *and* a pear from consecutive trees.

71 ABLE-BODIED

——You can begin anywhere, Taft Merryweather says to Martin Fugat. But you'll always end in the same place you started.

——Circle, Circle-Tangent, Circle, Abbot Ezra says cueing Martin Fugat to initiate the sequence.

Martin Fugat blindly opens the Dictionary on the counter-top.

——*Atlas*, Martin Fugat says. The Titan who stands on the Western Earth and balances the firmament on his shoulders.

——That's the Circle, Abbot Ezra says. Abe Hendrik, you're next.

——*Job* is the Hasidic Atlas, Abe Hendrik claims. But, for me, he's stronger than his Greek counterpart. He bore God's kingdom *plus* the Devil's kingdom on his fragile back.

——And there's the making of our Circle-Tangent, Abbot Ezra says. Gordon Flannery, continue.

——Currently, Gordon Flannery says, Pope Benedict is the representation of our Christian Job. Every successor of *Saint Peter* is known as the foundation of the Catholic Church.

——Circle-Tangent, Abbot Ezra says. Dale Rutherford, keep turning the Wheel.

——Peter is the patron saint of horology, Dale Rutherford imparts. He governs the manufacturing of *chronometers*.

——Which includes water-clocks, Issak Kidwell says. Also called the *klepsydra* or the *horologium ex aqua*.

——Still Circle-Tangent, Abbot Ezra says.

——Neptune and Poseidon, Simon Warner adds. The mythological Gods of water and *earth-quakes*.

Bewildered by this game of connections, Hugo Gustafson raises his hand.

——What causes earth-quakes? Hugo Gustafson asks.

——Return to the Circle, Taft Merryweather innocently hints.

Abbot Ezra points to Silas Paul.

——*Atlas shrugging*, Silas Paul says to Hugo.

72 ¹ABLE-BODIED SEAMAN

The extended Mantra for a future Trans-Benedictine Quantum Priest-hood.

——With their clothes on, the Devil snorts, girls smell like licorice and apricots. With their clothes off, aquariums. Boys smell like musk and ivory over pickles and boiled onions.

——Still, Silas Paul says to the Devil, Quantum Catholics claim that all flowers are of the edible sort. Which is God's way of allowing us to internalize the impossibly beautiful.

——For Quantum Catholics, Taft Merryweather says, a woman's body is speckled with reclusive buttercups; also known as canary brushes, cottage lights, or sun-feathers. Her petals feel wet, but are only cold, and own the taste of a deep flavored wheat. Her grasses arc just tall enough to allow the wind to tilt them; bringing the fragrance of honey-dew, black pepper, creek-water, and snails.

——Likewise, Silas Paul says, a man's body is nocturnal; but at night blows the hypnotizing perfume of vegetables, sweet lotions, and cashew butter. His long, supple goldenrods appear to need a nap, but lazily loft the cross-aroma of cinnamon and oranges.

——Early on, Taft Merryweather says to Silas Paul, the Devil taught if the feminine was in the air, one must love like a bird. The consequence has been a repetitive dream: a lilac that tastes like a woman's neck, but mixed with the presence of fore-skin.

[2]ABLE-BODIED SEAMAN

——Storming for forty days and forty nights, Simon Warner says pulling blankets up to Hugo's chin. That would require an enormous amount of *in-door beauty*.

——If I was Noah's son, Hugo Gustafson says, I would have lobbied before the flood and convinced him to bring along extra sets of jonquils and butterflies.

——Just a single pair for such a long and dangerous journey would have been depressing, Simon Warner admits.

——Jonquils and butterflies, Hugo Gustafson whimpers drifting into an ocean of sleep.

——*Bon voyage* my little mariner, Simon Warner says kissing Hugo on the fore-head.

73 [1]ABLOOM

A contest of metaphor. This weeks topic chosen by Hugo Gustafson: *Flowers*.

Fourth prize: Issak Kidwell
——A well-lit insect brothel, Issak Kidwell answers.
Third prize: Taft Merryweather
——Winter in a casket, Taft Merryweather answers.
Second prize: Abbot Ezra Davenport
——Summer poked upwards, Abbot Ezra answers.
First prize: Gordon Flannery
——*Vertical touching elliptical*, Gordon Flannery answers.

[2]ABLOOM

——Along exposed coasts that receive the full brunt of wave action, Taft Merryweather says, a *rocky intertidal* ecosystem replaces the salt marsh. Flowering plants are few in the rocky intertidal zone, but they include surf grass, a relative of other sea grasses more commonly found in quieter harbor waters. Many seaweeds and a few kelps are also attached to rocks in this habitat, each at its own particular depth within the intertidal zone. The different depths at which they are distributed probably reflect different degrees of adaptation to the stresses of exposure.

——*Fundamentalism*, Silas Paul insinuates.

74 ¹ABLUTED

——Thomas Aquinas and Augustine of Hippo, Dale Rutherford says, came upon one another after Yeshua's return. They were exploring the streets of Ambrojjio, mesmerized by how a Mosque and Yeshiva could be connected by beautiful Japanese bridges, like the ones that are seen in Monet's painting. The two saints erected a tent near the ocean and assembled a table on which they placed the Bibles they were peddling. Unaware of the tide, they began to build sand-castles for entertainment. After sun-set, two pre-pubescent girls in one-piece bathing suits approached the table. The pair of theologians winked at each other, failing to recognize that both damsels were *tulkus* of Jesus.

"Come to the edge and I'll wash your feet," Augustine said to the tulkus.

"Or bathe with the jelly-fish and I'll baptize you," Aquinas proposed over-riding Augustine.

Both girls opted for baptism on one condition: *All Bibles were to be dumped into the Atlantic.*

——Every book made waves in four directions, Martin Fugat says. *Common, Special, Solitary, and Perfect.*

²ABLUTED

——Ex Oriente, lux! Taft Merryweather chants.

75 ¹ABLUTION

Simon Warner and Abe Hendrik soak in the *caldarium* while composing a fable about Hugo Gustafson.

——When Hugo believes that he's half fish, Simon Warner says, and tires of opossum femurs as relics from the hands of Saint Augustine, there is only one thing left that interests him: *the daydreams of an aqueduct.*

——He cares nothing for the diamond vigor of a frowning arch, Abe Hendrik says.

——Or for a tedious break-down of the superstructure into a bland anthology of curves and triangles.

——Hugo prefers, Abe Hendrik says, to consider the pipeline a twelve mile stretch of drowning purgatory.

——But relishes the thought, Simon Warner says, of drinking the domesticated rain until his body swells like an elastic toad and sinks into the moss below the cat-tails.

——Buddhists say that this turns Hugo into a treasure chest.

——Thus, Simon Warner says, a symbol for an epoch.

²ABLUTION

——As fetuses, we started out life at ninety-nine percent, Gordon Flannery says.

——But when we were born, Dale Rutherford responds, this number had dropped to ninety percent.

——By the time we reached adulthood, Gordon Flannery adds, the percentage had faded to seventy.

——And if we die of old age, Dale Rutherford says, the final count will be around fifty percent.

——So what you're trying to say, Abbot Ezra interrupts, is throughout our lives, *humans exist mostly as water.*

76 ABNAKI

——Bodhidharma felt *ancient* when he dangled his mind from the tips of his hip-bones, Silas Paul says.

——Which doesn't mean *old* in the average sense of rings on a tree, Issak Kidwell confirms. It means *ancient* in the sense of the image of a tree that hibernates deep in the memory of a seed.

——They called him a sorcerer, a magician, a mystic, and a seer, Silas Paul says.

——But Bodhidharma responded with an ocean of composure. His favorite adage to his students was: *My Beloveds, We only know what we know.*

——Which turned out to be more than a feeling, Silas Paul says.

——One he equated with the assurance of a perennial flower.

——But mixed with the horrors of a night-time jungle.

——And the curious heart of a laughing child.

——Some days he celebrated, Issak Kidwell says, by pretending religion was nudity in the sun, and philosophy was who would hunt and who would gather.

——But even then, Silas Paul says, the *moon* was too young and too difficult.

——So according to Bodhidharma, Issak Kidwell says, growing into a god is mostly therapeutic.

——But after the womb, Silas Paul says, attempting to become an exalted human is merely to become an imposter.

77 ¹ABNEGATE

——*The Circle of Gardens*, Taft Merryweather says. They were vending flowers in the haze of the half-light.

——In a word, Abe Hendrik says, *Carnivalistic.*

——But don't forget the vault of butterflies, Hugo Gustafson pleads.

They were spreading around the germs of a joy-filled plague.

——Two progressive thoughts, Issak Kidwell requests.

——*Nimbus*, Martin Fugat says. Abbot Ezra's twenty-first century fashion statement.

——*Antinomian*, Taft Merryweather continues. Failure to realize real kisses don't begin with lips.

Issak Kidwell cheers.

——It's in there Brother Merryweather, Hugo Gustafson says. You just have to become it.

——Become what? Taft Merryweather asks.

A meadow-lark shuffles across the edges of the festive sky.

——Brother Merryweather, Hugo Gustafson says with a boyish smirk. Your cosmology...of *smiles*.

[2]ABNEGATE

——The most common form of prayer is petition or supplication, Dale Rutherford says to Gordon Flannery.

——*Begging*, Gordon Flannery clarifies. An example of living but not understanding.

——Like scratching a rock with a cloud, Abbot Ezra says. Living but not understanding.

78 [1]ABNEGATION

——Religion attempts to be scientific, Abbot Ezra says to Taft Merryweather.

——And science attempts to be philosophic, Taft Merryweather responds.

——And philosophy attempts to be religious, Simon Warner says to Abbot Ezra.

——All three are guilty of *category errors*, Abbot Ezra says. They strive to place their lens over the improper Eye.

——Science, Dale Rutherford says, sees the world through the Eye of Flesh which is empirical and monological.

——Philosophy, Abe Hendrik says, sees the world through the Eye of Reason which is rational and dialogical.

——Religion, Martin Fugat says, sees the world through the Eye of Contemplation which is mystical and translogical.

——So science, Silas Paul says, should stay within the boundaries of empirical fact.

——And philosophy, Issak Kidwell says, should stay within the boundaries of philosophical and psychological insight.

——Which leaves religion, Gordon Flannery says, to stay within the boundaries of *spiritual wisdom.*

[2]ABNEGATION

——Without a jot of philosophy left, Silas Paul says,
I let my nature flow where it will.
There are ten days of rice in my bag.
And, by the hearth, a bundle of firewood.
Who prattles of illusion or nirvana?
Forgetting the equal dusts of science and religion,
Listening to the night rain on the roof of my hut,
I sit at ease;
Both legs stretched out.

79 [1]ABNORMAL

Martin Fugat spinning his prayer wheel.

——Not so long ago, Issak Kidwell says, there were rat-killing dogs known as *Red Guards.* A government would bet on a Red Guard; how many rats he would kill. The rats were confined in a circular arena too high for a rat to jump over. But thankfully, the rats formed *pyramids* which allowed some of the top rats to amazingly escape.

——Just say it, Martin Fugat says with tears welling in his eyes.

——Poor Tibet, Issak Kidwell whispers.

[2]ABNORMAL

——Rat-singer? Hugo Gustafson says. Are you telling me Pope Benedict is an entertainer of rodents?

——All God's creatures great and small, Simon Warner says.

[3]ABNORMAL

Glorious Saint Augustine, Angel
Of Christianity,
During the opulence of Shrove Tuesday
Sat in a field of toad-stools
Confessing his Love
And admiration for the Christian
Religion.
Never in all his silent
Iambs could he have predicted he'd
Vanquish Thomas
Aquinas then
Lift him to God's
Glory by
Opining that their own
Deaths were
Something they should *practice* together.
Respecting the partial nature
Of this truth and
Care, We as the

Kosmos
Salute him.

80 ¹ABNORMALITY

——The architectural elements of the Taj Mahal, Silas Paul says, represent the gradual unfolding of matter to mind to spirit.

——In a Muslim-Hindu blend, Taft Merryweather says. Muhammad's *isra* and *mi'raj* are melted into the surface of Vedanta.

——And then Vedanta, Abe Hendrik says, is annexed to the ladder of Muhammad's excursion at twilight.

——Let's begin from the bottom with the *dadoes*, Silas Paul says. The decorative sculpted panels that line the lower walls of the Taj.

——*Annamayakosa*, Taft Merryweather interrupts.

——Above these panels, Silas Paul says re-taking the lead, a marble *arch* inflates itself until its peak can be considered the mid-riff of the façade.

Taft Merryweather blinks.

——And around the curvature of this arch, Abe Hendrik says, is a rectangular sheath called the *spandrel*.

——*Pranamayakosa* and *manomayakosa*, Taft Merryweather says.

——Slightly higher still is the *drum*, Silas Paul continues. A vertical wall which supports a dome or cupola.

Taft Merryweather blinks.

——In this case it's a *dome*, Abe Hendrik says. The onion dome is the largest outer dome of the tomb.

——*Vijnanamayakosa* and *anandamayakosa*, Taft Merryweather says.

——And finally comes the apex, Silas Paul says. The crowning adornment of a gilded *finial*.

Abe Hendrik blinks.

——*Fanaa*, Taft Merryweather says. The *prajna* of Muslims.

[2]ABNORMALITY

——Is the Taj Mahal a symbol for Sikhs and the *Guru Granth Sahib?* Hugo Gustafson asks.

——No, Martin Fugat responds. *But it should be.*

81 [1]ABNORMAL PSYCHOLOGY

Gordon Flannery teaching about the confusion of interiors and exteriors.

——Christianity's first casualties for the faith, Gordon Flannery says, automatically became its first recognized saints. Stephen, who was stoned to death in 35 c.e., is traditionally held to be the first Christian saint. Not one of the original apostles, he was one of the seventy-two original disciples of Christ, and was accused by pious Jews of preaching blasphemy. Taken before a hostile court, he preached a fiery sermon of astonishing power, ending with a vision of Jesus standing at the right hand of God in Heaven. This so inflamed the court that all formalities of a trial were forgotten and his accusers drove him outside the city and stoned him to death. His supposed grave was discovered in 415 at Kafa Gamala and his relics, including the *stones* used in his murder, were transferred to Constantinople, then to Rome. The word "martyr" is from the Greek *martus*, meaning *Witness*. And the verb form, *marturein*, means *to testify*.

[2]ABNORMAL PSYCHOLOGY

——The year Michelangelo died, Shakespeare was born, Hugo Gustafson says. Does this qualify as metempsychosis?

——Something like that, Simon Warner says.

82 [1]ABO

Dale Rutherford quoting Thomas Merton in his Sunday homily.

——In the first two chapters of the first Epistle to the Corinthians, Dale Rutherford says, Saint Paul distinguishes between two kinds of wisdom: one which consists in the knowledge of words and statements, a rational, dialectical wisdom, and another which is at once a matter of paradox and of experience, and goes beyond the reach of reason. To attain to this spiritual wisdom, one must first be liberated from servile dependence on the "wisdom of speech." This liberation is effected by the "word of the Cross" which makes no sense to those who cling to their own familiar views and habits of thought and is a means by which God "destroys the wisdom of the wise." The word of the Cross is in fact completely baffling and disconcerting both to the Greeks with their philosophy and to the Jews with their well-interpreted Law. But when one has been freed from dependence on verbal formulas and conceptual structures, the Cross becomes a source of "power." This power emanates from the "foolishness of God" and also makes use of "foolish instruments." On the other hand, he who can accept this paradoxical "foolishness" experiences in himself a secret and mysterious power, which is the power of Christ living in him as the ground of a totally new life and new being.

Hugo Gustafson grabs three of his mother's fingers.

——The Passion, Hugo Gustafson says, means the same as the First Noble Truth.

Hugo's mother nods.

——Suffering, Dale Rutherford says from the rostrum.

^{2}ABO

——Pronounce Muslim with a soft 's', Abbot Ezra says to Hugo Gustafson. Not with a 'z'.

83 ABOARD

——From Jerusalem, Abbot Ezra says, the world has learned that there are two definitions for romance.

——The first, Silas Paul says, is taught as a kind of pocket-knife that whittles nature into fables.

——For instance, Martin Fugat says, when a lagoon holds a gondola on its shoulders, that's team-work.

——And when the toadstools and desert truffles grow from the shadows of damp cobbles, Abe Hendrik says, that's perseverance.

——And when a seine pulls a mess of craw-fish and hellgrammites into the sun, Taft Merryweather says, that's religion.

——And when a tom-cat stays with his rag-doll kittens, Gordon Flannery says, that's family.

——As for the rest of life's lessons, they come later, Issak Kidwell says.

——Because for now in Jerusalem, Abbot Ezra says, touching lips with the Face of God is unfathomable.

84 ¹ABO BLOOD GROUP

Dictating the opening lines of The Quantum Heart Sutra.

——The Child Rabbinical Orchid was standing in The Field of Sculptures at Ambroggio along with a great community of Quantum Catholics and a great community of Asian and European bodhisattvas, and at that time, the Child Rabbinical Orchid fully entered (albeit briefly) the meditative concentration on the varieties of phenomena called The Full Moon Soul and The Five-Chambered Heart. At that very time as well, holy Ezra Davenport, the first abbot of Rainbow Abbey, the great being, the priest of private allegory, beheld the practice *itself* of The Five-Chambered Heart, and hence observed the skandhas as empty of inherent nature. Thereupon, through the Child Orchid's inspiration, the venerable Silas Paul spoke to holy Abbot Ezra, the great being, the priest of private allegory, and said, "Any noble son or daughter who wishes to engage The Five-Pointed Star of The Five-Chambered Heart should train in what contemplative practice?"

Form is empty, emptiness is form.

——The authentic injunction of one's choice, Taft Merryweather says.

²ABO BLOOD GROUP

——Will blood from an A positive Muslim donor, Hugo Gustafson asks, function in the body of an A positive Christian recipient?

——Without question, Simon Warner needlessly answers.

85 ¹ABODE

——From the journals of Lorenzo Gozzoli, Issak Kidwell says. Turn to September 5, 1459.

Silas Paul scans the page.

——The basement of the Sixth Mansion, Silas Paul says. The Dark Night of the Soul.

——Let's read it aloud, Issak Kidwell says. You first.

——*My tongue and my lips could have made pink strips for the landing of the wettest rain.*

——*And my hands, although small, could have warped steel beams into the dew that perks up on a morning basilica.*

——*But wrinkles in my skin had begun to emerge into a mid-life altar-call.*

——*And thoughts of duration had begun to un-fold as a nuisance in my attic and crawl-space of time.*

——*So I, a devoted Catholic, settled like a manufactured gnome in the garden of my choice.*

——*And after dipping sour tongs into the instincts of local carnivores, I constructively wallowed in an outward monotony—*

——*Which for me was creative.*

——*Like I lived in the veins of a sun-flower.*

——*For five deceptive years, being tethered to this hermitage was identity.*

——*And now that it's gone, even the birds in flight are an un-steady carapace for the beautiful.*

——*I stepped from the deck and saw Light in the river.*

——*But the river stayed murky.*

——*Like the cream in the color of an English tea.*

——*Then I wandered to the bank and saw fish in the river.*

——*But the fish stayed the color of a Japanese tea.*

——*So I dropped to the grass and saw myself in the river.*

——*But my image disappeared.*

——*Like the taste of the water in an Indian tea.*

——*Being planted in the Abbey was like candy to my leaves.*

——*It turned my mind into the wings of a whiskey-soaked butterfly.*

——*But living like a tree is a butter-scotch reality.*

——*A cinnamon solution.*

——*For a pepper-mint dream.*

²ABODE

Mark, six: thirty-one.

——Come by yourselves, Abe Hendrik says, to an out-of-the way place and rest for a while.

86 ¹ABOIL

——Although Lao Tzu, founder of Taoism, Abe Hendrik says, was the first important Chinese to penetrate the causal realm (which he called the "Tao"), his school never flowered as a method of actual practice and real sadhana, but tended—perhaps because he was too far ahead of his time in China—to degenerate, in the hands of his less evolved followers, into forms of magical and mythical rituals or, at best, into mere yogic techniques. But Lao Tzu himself stands forever as part of a historic elite: Christ, Buddha,

Lao Tzu, and the Upanishadic authors- the first great explorers of the Dharmakaya. The very best of Lao Tzu was, however, taken up almost entirely by Zen Buddhism, so that, in Zen, the best of the Buddha and the best of Lao Tzu not only lived on but flourished magnificently. Such, exactly, was the brilliance of Zen: Buddha and Lao Tzu combined and preserved.

²ABOIL

——The commercial exploitation, Gordon Flannery says, of Asia was made possible by the discovery of precious minerals in the West.

87 ABOLISH

——Everyone is similar, Abbot Ezra says.

——And every thing's prolific.

——But only if the mediation between now and forever, Taft Merryweather says.

——Becomes forever only.

——So when Hugo Gustafson yells, Martin Fugat says, "What about the god of the Arab frontier? What about the gods of the Ganges?".

——Quantum Catholics understand that the cry from an impatient angel is always serious.

——But we also understand there's a danger in the comfort and logical richness of monopoly on benevolence.

So it's Abe Hendrik who points out the obvious:

——*Even prophets infest their under-garments on a microscopic scale*!

88 ABOLITION

——Tell me who you *are*, Silas Paul says to Hugo Gustafson. Not who you *were*.

89 [1]ABOLITIONISM

——The production of interstellar dust particles, Dale Rutherford says, provides an essential first step on the road to planets. This holds true not only for solid planets like our own but also for gas-giant planets, typified in the Sun's family by Jupiter and Saturn. Even though these planets consist primarily of hydrogen and helium, astrophysicists have concluded from their calculations of the planets' internal structure, along with their measurements of the planets' masses, that the gas giants must have solid cores. Of Jupiter's total mass, 318 times Earth's, several dozen Earth masses reside in a solid core. Saturn, with ninety-five times Earth's mass, also has a solid core with one or two dozen times the mass of the Earth. The Sun's two smaller gas-giant planets, Uranus and Neptune, have proportionately larger solid cores. In these planets, with fifteen and seventeen times Earth's mass, respectively, the core may contain more than half of the planet's mass.

Lightning strikes the island of Ambrojjio.

——Are you resting in infinity, Hugo Gustafson asks Dale Rutherford. Corresponding thunder.

——Resting *as* infinity, Dale Rutherford corrects Hugo.

[2]ABOLITIONISM

——Selenium comes from *selene*, Dale Rutherford says, the Greek word for the moon, so named because this element was always found in association with the element tellurium, which had already been named for Earth, from the Latin *tellus*.

——Let's take deep breaths together as we swallow the moon! Silas Paul exclaims.

[3]ABOLITIONISM

Glorious Erwin Schroedinger, Angel

Of Esotericism,

During the rigors of Autumn Equinox

Surveyed the lifestyles of sub-atomic

Components

Automatically resisting temptation to

Reject the

Non-dual

Invitations of

Vedanta.

Attraction to this

Logos is a

Gentle guarding

Of an old-fashioned

Dynamic: Electrons and

Shamanism mutually arising.

Respecting the partial nature

Of this truth and

Care, We as the

Kosmos

Salute him.

90 ¹ABOMASUM

——When she was invisible, Silas Paul says.

——Blinking eyes in a tree trunk or a pea stem.

——Before she accomplished her whirling body, Taft Merryweather
says.

——Before the return of pearl eyes to an oyster shell.

Discoid flowers of tansy.

——When noon's intensity wrapped her circle, Abbot Ezra says.

——Rounding her for the passive tangent.

——When the apple tree dropped sweet auburn.

Discoid flowers of tansy.

——When yesterday's progeny breath together, Issak Kidwell says.

——One pulling in and one pushing out.

——When the old fears prove true.

Discoid flowers of tansy.

²ABOMASUM

——The earliest documentary evidence, Silas Paul says, for the existence of animal homes in India occurs during the reign of Ashoka (third century b.c.e.), the Mauryan ruler whose empire covered the entire Indian subcontinent with the exception of a few states in the extreme south of the peninsula. Ashoka adopted Buddhism as the imperial state religion, and the basic tenets of the religion were proclaimed throughout the empire. Several of these official proclamations were engraved on stone pillars scattered around the country, surviving for posterity. Two of these, Rock Edict I and Pillar Edict V, specifically prohibit the slaughter of animals.

91 ¹A-BOMB

Three Laws of Thermodynamics.

——Energy can neither be created nor destroyed, Gordon Flannery says.

——*Esoteric Religion*, Silas Paul responds.

——Energy systems have a tendency to increase their entropy rather than decrease it, Gordon Flannery says.

——*Agnosticism*, Silas Paul responds.

——As temperature approaches absolute zero, the entropy of a system approaches a constant, Gordon Flannery says.

——*Exoteric Religion*, Silas Paul responds.

[2]A-BOMB

——The *relative ego* is equivalent to fission, Abe Hendrik says.

——The *transcendental ego* is equivalent to fusion, Simon Warner replies.

92 ABOMINABLE

Items presented by Hugo Gustafson for show and tell: dandelion bracelets and tiaras, a worn out horseshoe, recipes for summer squash and zucchini, a terrarium, silt from the Jordan River, a turtle shell, a statue of Ganesha, mill-worms and a cane pole, a fox carcass, signatures from Chinese gentry, Taft Merryweather's zafu and zabuton, a portrait of Ramana Maharshi, a cardboard model of the Dome of the Rock, a lunar calendar, a puzzling fossil of a trilobite, an alms bowl, an ode to the Mahayana, a cuneiform tablet, sketches of Constantinople, and finally, blue-skinned Martin, naked from the waste up, pleading with ten toes in the posies:

——*Please think of me as your halogen fire-fly, or better yet, your friend.*

93 [1]ABOMINABLE SNOWMAN

Six deviations from Mahamudra.

——Not understanding, Taft Merryweather says, that the mind-essence is the *unity of appearance and emptiness* endowed with the supreme of all aspects, the unobstructed interdependence of cause and effect, one slips into focusing on the empty aspect. This fault is called 'basic straying from the essence of emptiness.'

——Similarly, Abe Hendrik says, after engaging in meditation, although one may have intellectually understood the meaning of the natural state, *experience* has not arisen in oneself. Or, again forgetting that which has arisen, the meaning will not be present within ones being, although one might be able to explain the words to others. This is called 'temporary straying from the essense.'

——While what is needed at present is the path itself, Issak Kidwell says, one desires to attain some other result at a later date. This is called 'basic straying from the path.'

——To regard, Gordon Flannery says, the sustaining of the ordinary wakefulness of ones mind as insufficient while one desires a magnificent mind-made meditation and then searches for it elsewhere is called 'temporary straying from the path.'

——When something such as a disturbing emotion arises, Martin Fugat says, not knowing how to take its essence as the path and instead to meditate on some other technique according to the lower vehicles is called 'basic straying from the remedy.'

——Not knowing, Dale Rutherford says, how to take whatever arises, such as a thought, as the path, but to block off that instance or having to destroy it before resting in meditation is called the deviation into the 'temporary straying from the remedy.'

[2]ABOMINABLE SNOWMAN

——The Himalayas are the highest mountain system in the world, Issak Kidwell says. They extend in an arc across central Asia from the north-eastern border of Afghanistan to the northwestern border of Burma, covering about two thousand miles. The Himalayas are oftern called the Himalaya, which means "abode of the snow" in Sanskrit.

——Divides India and Tibet, Hugo Gustafson says.

——Connects them, Simon Warner corrects.

94 [1]ABOMINATE

Selections from the journals of Erasmus Grunewald (1461) in Silas Paul's phylactery.

——Samsara. Nirvana. Then back to Samsara, Silas Paul says.

The trees of the winter forest/
   look like wetted boxes.
They make me think
        of the words/
  'arlington'
AND
  'cemetery'.
(I don't know why).

[2]ABOMINATE

The red eye/
of a curved thrasher.
The contracted perch/
of a stumpy wren.
The frowning stare/
of a black warbler.
Nothing can be anything.
      (else).

[3]ABOMINATE

I have seen the majesty of a grand fir,
shagged with the busts
      of a dozen mothers.
Their nests so close,
the rearers que in airobatic lines,
waiting their turn to release
a morsel of worm or live cricket.
  (into a bald open beak).

95 ABOMINATION

——There is something romantic about playing symbiosis with a disc in the sky, Taft Merryweather says.

——The problem, Dale Rutherford responds, is that some humans feel like parasites.

——Right now if it was possible, Abbot Ezra says, there are people who would flood their lungs, not their throats, with the river.

——Disturbingly, Issak Kidwell says, the indication is that the majority has become the product of insufficient knowledge.

——And remain unaware of their contribution to the design which lurks in the greenery.

——Once again, Simon Warner says, enlightenment proves to include intuition.

——So everyone exhales, Gordon Flannery says, littering the ground with a necessity.

——This is part of the unknown they are searching for.

——The light pours in and Earth flourishes, Dale Rutherford says.

——*Most claim the globe is just a place*, Silas Paul points out.

——But not everybody, Martin Fugat responds.

——Not yet, Taft Merryweather adds.

——And hopefully not ever.

96 ABORAL

——If only he could pickle this moment with a dose of light.

——Forget the rain in December turns a wagon's wheel in June.

——Forget thistles and the disillusion.

——Forget spring.

——But not everyone, Simon Warner says, can ease their spade into the earth and strike reality.

——So Taft Merryweather, Abe Hendrik says, reactivates two pesticides for the literal word.

——*Sleep* and *imagination*.

——He crinkles up his forehead and shouts:

——*Where are all the sensitive plants?! The water lilies, the pineapples, the palm trees?!*

——Then he laughs because he finds them.

——Rainbow Abbey will never be a tropical paradise, Simon Warner says.

——It's trapped into the life of an over-sized toad-stool submerged to its under-belly.

——Never will nine flowers blossom into nine vials of sugar for the honey-bee.

——Never, Abe Hendrik says, will a silver trout pose as a second moon.

——But for Taft Merryweather, Simon Warner says, even if just for an instant, all things are possible.

——Especially his ability to translate the breeze.

97 ABORIGINAL

Silas Paul and Martin Fugat feeding zebras at the Hall of Vertebrates.

——Irrational osmosis can penetrate my mind like a thousand templars! Silas Paul exclaims.

——But every thought confirms the joke of biological unfoldings!

98 [1]ABORIGINE

Chandogya Upanishad.

——Space is greater than heat. In it are both the sun and the moon, lightning, the constellations, and fire. Through space one calls, through space one hears, through space one replies; in space one takes pleasure, in space one does not take pleasure, in space one is born, into space one grows.

Worship space.

——The one who worships space as *brahman* achieves spacious worlds, clear, unobstructed, with plenty of room to move. He wins freedom to move as far as space can go - the one who worships space as *brahman*.

——Blessed one, is there anything greater than space?

——There *is* something greater than space.

——Tell me about it blessed one.

²ABORIGINE

——I'm not satisfied with secrets of hope, Abe Hendrik shouts.

——Or with the docile acceptance of darkness as solution.

——For me, Abe Hendrik says, long ago the world had mastered the ability to regenerate the outward landscape.

——And to change it into a place where smells have color and colors have sound.

——So at worst, Abe Hendrik says, if the world quits turning, it will only sink further into the table of space.

——Then it will compensate, Silas Paul says. Like a blind man's brain.

——Inducing the breath of design that reinvigorates the seasons.

99 ¹ABORNING

——As Sunday afternoon wriggles its way into the imaginations of the northern hemispheres, Abbot Ezra says.

——Simon and Hugo, Gordon Flannery says, dreaming at a table-top in the perfect light, weave themselves into a pair of anonymous chairs and dabble their curious tongues into idle cups of bubbling coffee.

——Simon says that such a caustic laziness is the ideal climate for thinkers.

——So Hugo inhales a certain spice about the Abbey air, Taft Merryweather says.

————One that flips him inside the Secluded Under.

————Forcing him to disappear into an ancient disembodied self.

————And to become a kosmic singularity among a council of unbelievers.

————Maybe Simon *is* right, Issak Kidwell says. Hugo is the navel of a cartwheel galaxy.

————But just in case he's not, Silas Paul says, he loses himself into the shade of the chapel-going parasols.

————And then has Hugo swear that if he ever dies, Martin Fugat says, they will search for one another at the base of a mystical tower.

————And then go skipping into heaven *together*.

²ABORNING

Glorious Dogen, Angel
Of Buddhism,
During the holiday of Vesak
Suddenly saw seven silver
Crows
Assemble his Soul into a
Raven.
Noting his new-fangled
Intensity, he marveled at the way
Virtual birds were
Annihilated by
Linking crows into
Greater
Orders of ravenous
D*epth* and
Splendor.
Respecting the partial nature
Of this truth and

Care, We as the
Kosmos
Salute him.

100 ABORT

Out of the house with his sketch-book immediately following a cooling summer rain, Hugo Gustafson sloshes to his favorite gazebo in The Field of Sculptures.

——I see rocks, Hugo Gustafson says to Silas Paul. But no carnival.

——That's because your seeing them with your eyes, Silas Paul responds. Not with your spiritual intelligence.

NOTES

ENTRY 1

1. **Axial** This is a reference to the Axial Age, a term coined by German philosopher Karl Jaspers to describe the period from 800 BCE to 200 BCE during which revolutionary thinking appeared simultaneously in China, India, and the Occident laying foundations for the futures of philosophy and religion.

2. **Sufi** An Islamic mystic who practices Sufism, a mystical tradition of Islam.

3. **Benedictines** Christian monks who subscribe to the Rule of St. Benedict of Nursia (ca. 480-547). In this instance, trans-Benedictine means beyond conventional Benedictine rule or a "post-Benedictine" rule. Taft Merryweather is aspiring to update what is already trans-Benedictine at Rainbow Abbey.

4. **Allahu akbar** Arabic for "God is most great". An Islamic exclamation called the *takbir*, a phrase frequently uttered in formal prayer and many other occasions.

5. **Sri Krishna** Sri is used as a title of veneration, a Hindu honorific stemming from the Vedic conception of prosperity. Krishna is the dark-complexioned god (frequently depicted with blue skin) often identified as an avatar (incarnation) of Vishnu, but for many Hindus more important than Vishnu himself.

6. **Lectio Divina** Latin for 'spiritual reading' representing an early monastic technique of prayer intended to achieve communion with God as well as provide special spiritual insights and peace. For a contemporary model of Lectio Divina see Father Thomas Keating's Centering Prayer movement.

7. **Muid ad-Din ibn al-Arabi** Sufi mystical philosopher (1165-1240).

8. **Rumi** Jalal ad-Din Muhammad Rumi, a thirteenth century Persian poet, jurist, and theologian. After his death, his followers founded the Mevlevi Order better known as the "Whirling Dervishes".

9. **Shariah** The religious law of Islam embracing the entire body of rules and moral directives that many Muslims believe God has ordained.

10. **The Scarlet Letter** A novel by American author Nathaniel Hawthorne published in 1850. This novel was referenced because of it's portrayal of pre-conventional and conventional moral attitudes as well as the importance of the letter 'A'.

11. **World-centric** A "level of consciousness, awareness, or moral development" which has transcended but included the previous stage of "ethnocentricity." A stage of human development able to experience the "World Soul".

12. **Stupa** A Buddhist monument, generally dome-shaped with towerlike structures on top. A number of stupas house what are believed to be physical remains of the Buddha.

13. **Zazen** Zen Buddhist seated meditation.

14. **Dervish** A Sufi mystic from the Mevlevi Order.

ENTRY 2

1. **Salat** The five daily ritual prayers that Muslims offer to God.

2. **Mass** Term used to describe celebration of the Eucharist in the Western liturgical rights of the Catholic Church (and other Protestant denominations).

3. **The Circle of Gardens** A botanical garden on the grounds of Rainbow Abbey reached by following red stepping stones branching from The Quantum Constructions (see Entry 36, Note 1.

4. **Saraswati** Hindu goddess of learning and the arts. Consort of Lord Brahma, the creator.

5. **Disporum trachycapum** The binomial name (genus and species) for fireweed. The binomial names which follow correspond to the common names spoken by Martin Fugat to which Taft Merryweather is responding.

6. **Taj Mahal** Marble tomb and place of pilgrimage in Agra, India. The shrine was constructed by the Muslim Moghul emperor Shah Jihan (d. 1666) to commemorate his consort, Mumtaz Mahal. The architecture fuses

Indian and Islamic styles.

7. **Balfour Declaration** A letter written by the British Foreign Office in 1917 (named after the British Lord President of the Council Arthur Balfour) which stated the British government viewed with favor the establishment in Palestine of a national home for the Jewish People.

8. **Triple Vision** A term taken from the preface of Karen Armstrong's book *Holy War: The Crusades and Their Impact on Today's World*.

ENTRY 3

1. **The Field of Sculptures** Acres of meadow designated for displaying the sculptures of Silas Paul and other artists of Rainbow Abbey's past. Found by following blue stepping stones branching from the Quantum Constructions. See Entry 2, Note 3 for a description of The Circle of Gardens.

2. **The Hall of Vertebrates** A zoo for rehabilitated animals on the grounds of Rainbow Abbey found by following yellow stepping stones from the Quantum Constructions.

3. **Three Jewels** The Three Jewels of Buddism: Buddha, Dharma, and Sangha which can also be compared to Plato's Beautiful, True, and Good and the pronouns I, It, and We.

ENTRY 4

1. **Melchizedek** Represents the priestly line through which a future king of Israel's Davidic line was ordained. Traditional Christianity believes that Jesus is the Messiah spoken of as "a priest forever in the order of Melchizedek" (Psalms 110: 4). Some Christians also claim the covenenant of Jesus is superior to the covenant of the Levitical priesthood.

2. **The Tao of Physics** A book by physicist Fritjof Capra.

3. **Vulgate** The Latin translation of the Bible by Jerome in the last decades of the fourth century. The Vulgate was confirmed as the official version of the Roman Catholic Church at the Council of Trent (1545-1563) and until 1943 all Roman Catholic translations were requried to use it.

4. **Seventy** Another name for the Septuagint, the earliest known Greek translation of the Hebrew Bible.

ENTRY 5

1. **Ehyeh-Asher-Ehyeh** Hebrew for "I am who I am" or "I am what I shall be".

2. **Tanakh** An acronym that identifies the Hebrew Bible. Based on the initial Hebrew letters of the text's three parts: Torah (Instruction), Nevi'im (Prophets), and Ketuvim (Writings).

3. **Elohim** In the Hebrew Bible, divine name translated as "God" in English.

4. **Yahweh** In the Hebrew Bible, divine name translated as "Lord" in English.

5. **Chakras** In Indic systems, vortexes of energy in the subtle body. In most systems there are six or seven chakras: base of the spine (muladhara), genitals (svadhishthana), navel (manipura), heart (anahata), throat (vishuddha), and between the eyebrows (ajna). The seventh or transcendent chakra above the head (sahasrara) is the terminus for subtle energy, called *kundalini*, that ascends from the muladhara up through the various chakras.

ENTRY 6

1. **Sura** One of 114 literary divisions or chapters in the Qur'an.

2. **Saint Francis** Francis of Assisi (ca. 1181-1226). Roman Catholic saint and founder of the Franciscan order.

3. **Zakat** The obligatory alms paid by self-sufficient adult Muslims to aid the Islamic community.

4. The prayer by Simon Warner is adapted from the *Canticle of the Sun*, a religious song composed by Saint Francis of Assisi.

5. **Third-tier consciousness** For a description of "levels of consciousness" see Don Beck's *Spiral Dynamics Integral* or Ken Wilber's *Boomeritis*.

6. **Recitation** Qur'an is Arabic for "The Recitation."

7. **King James** An English translation of the Bible commissioned by King James I of Englan and published in 1611.

ENTRY 7

1. **Musa** Arabic for Moses.

2. **Yeshua** Hebrew or Aramaic for Jesus.

3. **Pali Canon** Standard scripture collection of the Theravada Buddhist tradition. Pali is the liturgical language in which the scriptures of Theravada Buddhism were written down in Sri Lanka in the first century BCE.

4. **Yahweh** See Entry 5, Note 4.

5. **Moses** The towering figure in the narrative of the Hebrew Bible who led Israel out of Egypt and transmitted God's commandments.

6. **Mosque** A site for assembly and worship for Muslims.

ENTRY 8

1. **Noah's Ark** Boat constructed by Noah to escape the Flood (Genesis 6:5-9:17).

2. **Prince Henry the Navigator** Prince of the Portuguese House of Aviz and an important figure in the early days of the Portuguese Empire and its exploration of the Atlantic Ocean and the African coast.

3. **Poseidon** Greek god of the sea and earthquakes.

4. **Lustrum** A ceremonial rite for Roman purification.

5. **Archimedes** Ancient Greek mathematician, physicist, engineer, astronomer, and philospher. Important here for his discovery of the Law of buoyancy.

6. **Krishna** See Entry 1, Note 5.

ENTRY 9

1. **Stigma** A part of the female orgaon of a flower, essentially the terminal part of a pistil

2. **Ox-herding pictures** A series of short poems accompanied by woodcuts that are intended to illustrate the stages of a Mahayana Buddhist

practitioner's progression towards enlightenment.

3. **Vespers** The evening prayer service in the Roman Catholic and Eastern Orthodox liturgies of the canonical hours.

4. **Carpel** The female reproductive organ of a flower.

5. **Tao** Chinese for "Way", a principle concept in traditional Chinese thought and religion.

ENTRY 10

1. **Five Pillars** Devotional acts required of all Muslims. All other difficult words or concepts in this entry are defined in the text.

2. **Minarets** Distinctive architectural features of Islamic mosques. They are generally tall, graceful spires, with onion-shaped crowns, usually either free standing or much taller than the surrounding support structure. One function of a minaret is to provide a vantage point from which the *muezzin* can call the faithful to prayer.

3. **Terce** A fixed time of prayer (9 a.m.) of the Divine Office of Christian liturgy.

4. **Dark Night of the Soul** A term used to describe a specific phase of a person's spiritual life. It is used as a metaphor to describe the experience of loneliness and desolation that can occur during spiritual growth. The term is taken from the writings of the Spanish poet and Roman Catholic mystic Saint John of the Cross.

ENTRY 11

1. **Menorah** A seven branched candelabrum to be lit by olive oil in the Tabernacle and the Temple in Jerusalem. It is one of the oldest symbols of the Jewish people.

2. **Crescent** A symbol of Islamic faith.

3. **Prince Henry** Prince Henry the Navigator. See Entry 8, Note 2.

4. **Prophet** Muhammad, the founder of Islam.

5. **Brahma** The creator deity in classical Hinduism. He is the personification and embodment of the sacred power of Vedic texts and rituals.

ENTRY 12

1. **Metazoans** A group comprising all animals except the Protozoa.

2. **Cambrian Explosion** Refers to the geologically sudden appearance in the fossil record of the ancestors of familiar animlas, starting about 542 million years ago.

3. **Orion Arm** A spiral arm of the Milky Way galaxy. The solar system and Earth are within the Orion Arm. The Virgo Supercluster is a galactic supercluster that contains the Milky Way galaxy.

4. **Cosmic Explosion** The Big Bang.

5. **Heraclitus** Pre-Socratic Greek philosopher. The names which follow in Dale Rutherford's comment are all great philosophers and or religious luminaries from the Axial Age.

6. **Axial Explosion** See Entry 1, Note 1.

ENTRY 13

1. **Waiting For Godot** A play by Samuel Beckett (published 1952).

ENTRY 14

1. This entry contains the first mention of Hugo Gustafson. He is just returning from summer camp in the United States.

2. **Solar Projection** A homemade device (usually made with a shoe box) used to view a solar eclipse.

3. **Leonardo** Leonardo da Vinci. Italian architect, sculptor, engineer, inventor, mathematician, and painter (1452-1519).

4. **Rimbaud** Arthur Rimbaud. French poet (1854-1891).

5. **Tolstoy** Leo Tolstoy. Russian novelist, essayist, philosopher, and Christian thinker (1828-1910).

6. **Gandhi** Mahatma Gandhi. Major political and spiritual leader of the Indian Independence movement (1869-1948).

7. **Mitochondrial Eve** Name given by researchers to the woman who is the matrilineal most recent commom ancestor for all living humans. The mitochondrial DNA in all living humans is derived from hers.

ENTRY 15

1. **Southern Baptist** Largest Protestant denomination in the United States.

2. **Benedict Sixteen** Pope Benedict XVI. Inaugurated April 24, 2005.

3. **Catholic Catechism** Official exposition of the teachings of the Catholic Church.

4. **Lolita** A novel by Vladimir Nabakov first published in 1955.

5. **Autobiography of Red** A verse novel by Anne Carson published in 1998.

6. **Hegel** German philosopher Georg Hegel (1770-1831).

ENTRY 16

1. **Neural Net** A computing paradigm that is loosely modeled after cortical structures of the brain.

2. **Original Testament** What Christians call the Old Testament of the Bible.

3. **Abraham** Ancestor of the Hebrews. In Jewish, Christian, and Islamic traditions Abraham is seen as a model of faith.

4. **Yahweh** See Entry 5, Note 4.

5. **Elohim** See Entry 5, Note 3.

6. **David** In the Hebrew Bible, king of Israel and Judea, fouder of the Judean royal dynasty. In Jewish and Christian tradition, the Messiah will be from the lineage of David.

7. **Allah** The foremost name for the supreme being according to Islamic belief. A term applied to God generally by Arabic speaking peoples, be they Muslims, Jews, or Christians.

8. Most of this entry was adapted from Jack Miles *A Biography of God* pp. 250-251.

ENTRY 17

1. **Recitation** See Entry 6, Note 6.

2. This entry is an interpretation of sura 101 providing insight into

"Triple Vision".

ENTRY 18

1. **Saladin** Twelfth century Kurdish Muslim general and warrior from Tikrit. He was renowned in both the Muslim and Christian worlds for his leadership and military prowess tempered by his chivalry and merciful nature during his war against the Crusaders.

2. **Kurdish** Ethnic group who consider themselves to be indigenous to a region often referred to as Kurdistan, an area which includes parts of Iran, Iraq, Syria, and Turkey.

3. **Saracen** People from the Saracen Empire. Used during the Crusades to refer to all Muslims.

4. **Tikrit** Saladin's home which is now located in Iraq about 140 km northwest of Baghdad.

5. **Ford Of Jacob's Daughters** Battle fought in 1179 between the Kingdom of Jerusalem and the forces of Saladin. The Battle of Hattin took place in 1187 between the same opponents.

ENTRY 19

1. **Eve** The first woman created in the Bible to be Adam's wife. This entry alludes to her actions in what is called the Temptation and the Fall.

2. **Lila** Means "play" (kosmic play) in Sanskrit. It is an important theological, dramaturgical, and aesthetic concept associated with Hinduism.

3. **Rabbi** Intellectual and spiritual leaders of the Jewish community.

ENTRY 20

1. **Ahmad ibn Majid** Arab navigator, cartographer, and poet born in 1421. It is argued that ibn Majid helped the Portuguese sailor Vasco Da Gama in completing the first all water trade route between Europe and India.

2. **Prince Henry the Navigator** See Entry 8, Note 2.

3. **Afonso V** King of Portugal (1432-1481).

4. **Pope Nicholas V** First humanist Pope. Held office from 1447 to 1455.

5. **Vatican** The leadership of the Roman Catholic Church. Vatican City is a sovereign city-state whose territory consists of a walled enclave within the city of Rome.

6. **Saint Paul** A first-century Jew who experienced himself called by God to be an apostle of Jesus Christ to the Gentiles (non-Jews) to assure them of their acceptance by God.

7. **Yahweh** See Entry 5, Note 4.

ENTRY 21

1. **Prophet Muhammad** See Entry 11, Note 4.

2. **Yeshua** See Entry 7, Note 2.

3. **Heterozygous** Used to describe a cell or organism that has two or more different versions (alleles) of at least one of its genes. The offspring of such an organism may thus differ with regard to the characteristics determined by the gene or genes involved, depending on which version of the gene they inherit.

4. **Homozygous** Having two identical genes at the corresponding loci of homologous chromosomes.

5. **Phenotype** Visible characteristics of an organism.

6. **Krishna** See Entry 1, Note 5.

7. **Methemoglobinemia** A genetic blood disorder characterized by the presence of a higher than normal level of methemoglobin in the blood which causes a blue tint to the skin.

ENTRY 22

1. **Benedictine** See Entry 1, Note 3.

2. **Dharma** The proper course of conduct, norm, the Buddhist religion, ultimate realities, ultimate principles. Dharma has been called "the central conception of Buddhism"; and the expression "the Dharma", or "Buddha-Dharma", is often used to mean Buddhism as a system of thought and

practice.

3. **Pidgin** Name given to any language created, usually spontaneously, out of a mixture of other languages as a means of communication between speakers of different tongues.

ENTRY 23

1. **Abbe H. Breuil** French archeologist. Generally known for his work on cave art.

2. **Mosque** See Entry 7, Note 6.

3. **Terce** See Entry 10, Note 3.

4. **Paleolithic** Early Stone Age.

5. **Semiotic** Semiotics or Semiology is the study of signs and symbols.

ENTRY 24

1. **Scriptorium** A room in a monastery for storing, copying, illustrating, or reading manuscripts.

2. **Lectio** Lectio Divina. See Entry 1, Note 6.

3. **Marian** Having to do with the Virgin Mary. Likewise for the reference to our "Blessed Lady".

4. **Muhammad** See Entry 11, Note 4.

5. **Fatima** The name of Muhammad's youngest daughter as well as a reference to "Our Lady of Fatima", a title given to the Virgin Mary by Catholics who believe she appeared monthly, for several months, to three shepherd children in Fatima, Portugal in 1917.

6. **Joseph** Husband of Mary and legal father of Jesus of Nazareth.

7. **Buddha** Siddhartha Gautama.

ENTRY 25

1. This entry is adapted from Ken Wilber's *Up From Eden: A Transpersonal View of Human Evolution* p. 70.

2. **Lascaux** A complex of caves in Southwestern France famous for its cave paintings.

3. **Salat** See Entry 2, Note 1.

4. **Yogi** One who practices yoga (mostly reserved for advanced practitioners).

5. **Lohengrin** Son of Parzival and knight of the Holy Grail.

6. **Templars** The Poor Knights of Christ and of the Temple of Solomon, a Catholic secret military order founded in the Latin Kingdom of Jerusalem in 1119.

7. **Gabriel** In Jewish and Christian sources, an archangel, best known in Christianity for the announcement to Mary that she was to bear Jesus. In Islam, Gabriel is the angel who conveys God's messages to humans, especially prophets. The Qur'an was brought by Gabriel to Muhammad and guided Muhammad during his Night Journey.

8. **Zen** The largest school of Buddhism in Japan focusing on methods for the attainment of enlightenment.

9. **Vedanta** The end or culmination of the Veda. Vedanta is the most influential traditional Hindu school of thought to the present day, especially in its non-dualistic form.

10. **Sufi** See Entry 1, Note 2.

11. **Cistercian** A Christian monastic order who are known to follow a stricter conformity to the Rule of St. Benedict.

12. **Tao** See Entry 9, Note 5.

13. **Sikh** An adherent of Sikhism.

ENTRY 26

1. **Pope Nicholas V** See Entry 20, Note 4.

2. **Oblate** A layperson who is part of a religious community.

3. **Trans-Benedictine** See Entry 1, Note 3.

ENTRY 27

1. **Abbot** The monk in charge of a monastery.

2. **Tao** See Entry 9, Note 5.

ENTRY 28

1. **The Field of Sculptures** See Entry 3, Note 1.

2. **Oblate** See Entry 26, Note 2.

3. **The Hall of Vertebrates** See Entry 3, Note 2.

4. **Zaid Haritha** Adopted son of the Prophet, Muhammad.

5. **Prophet's wife** Muhammad's first wife, Khadija.

6. **Atman** Philosophical term used in Hinduism, Vedanta, and Buddhism to identify the soul or the ego.

7. **Brahman** In Hindu philosophy, the absolute and unified ground of all being.

ENTRY 29

1. **Vishnu** In Hinduism, the pervading protector of the universe.

2. **Buddha** See Entry 24, Note 7. Sometimes considered the ninth avatar of Vishnu.

3. **Obadiah** Author of the Book of Obadiah in both the Hebrew and Christian Bibles. Abdias is Latin for Obadiah.

4. **Yeshua** See Entry 7, Note 2.

5. **Neo-cortex** The roof of the cerebral cortex that forms the part of the mammalian brain that has evolved most recently and makes possible higher brain function.

6. **Concrete Operational** A mode of cognition which involves the capacity to form mental rules and to take mental roles.

ENTRY 30

1. **Fire blight** A contagious bacterial disease affecting apples, pears, and other members of the family Rosaceae.

2. **Cowl** A monk's hooded cloak.

3. **Chakras** See Entry 5, Note 5.

4. **Samsara** An Indic term for the cycle of birth and death or the "ordinary" spatio-temporal world.

5. For a description of Ox-herding pictures see Entry 9, Note 2.

ENTRY 31

1. **Chakras** See Entry 5, Note 5.

2. **Adam** In the Bible, the first man created by God. Father of Cain and Abel.

3. **Cain and Abel** The sons of Adam and Eve.

4. **Iblis** Iblis and all the figures in Martin Fugat's statement are equivalent to the Christain Devil.

5. **Mephistopheles** In medieval mythology, a subordinate to the Devil.

6. **Mark** The gospel of Mark.

7. **Shiva** Hindu God of destruction.

8. **Siddhartha** The Buddha.

9. **Confucius** Chinese thinker and social philosopher (551-479 BCE).

10. **Poseidon** See Entry 8, Note 3.

11. **Vishnu** See Entry 29, Note 1.

ENTRY 32

1. **Binary Code** A computer code that uses the binary number system.

2. **Iberian** From the Iberian Peninsula.

3. **Yahweh** See Entry 5, Note 4.

ENTRY 33

1. **Josaphat** Said to have lived and died in third or fourth century India. His story appears to be in many repects a Christianized version of Gautama Buddha's story.

2. **Athanasius** Athanasius of Alexandria. Roman Catholic saint considered one of thirty-three doctors of the Church (293-372).

3. **Augustine** Saint Augustine of Hippo (354-430).

4. **Mahayana** Branch of Buddhism which includes Tibetan, Chinese, and Zen.

5. **Manichee** Manichaeism. A major ancient religion of Iranian origin.

6. **Basho** Matsuo Basho (1644-1694). Most famous poet of the Edo period in Japan.

7. **Formal Operation** As in "formal operational cognition". A mode of cognition that can operate on thought itself (transcends and includes Concrete Operation; See Entry 29, Note 6).

8. **Aperspectival** A term used by Jean Gebser in regards to the awareness of "vision-logic". "Aperspectival madness" is a term used to describe the belief that all truth is relative.

ENTRY 34

1. The monk-poets listed in the initial paragraph were chosen by Giovanni Landino, the first "manager" of Rainbow Abbey appointed by Pope Nicholas V. The words in parentheses are successive levels of spiritual awareness in Kabbalah.

2. **Oporto** City in Portugal associated with Prince Henry the Navigator. The first monk-poets of Rainbow Abbey meet at Oporto before setting sail for the Isle of Man (Ambrojjio).

3. **Yeshua** See Entry 7, Note 2.

4. **Franciscan** See Entry 6, Note 2.

ENTRY 35

1. The Latin translated to English roughly means: "Rainbow Abbey is a place not made by human hands." The second part translated means: "A secluded place for the soul to grow."

2. **Rosary** An important and traditional devotion of the Roman Catholic Church consisting of a set of prayer beads and a system of set prayers.

3. **Redactor** The figure who assembled hypothetical source texts of the Torah into a single work.

4. **Torah** The first five books of the Tanakh: Genesis, Exodus, Leviticus, Numbers, and Deutoronomy.

5. **Gitas** The Bhagavad Gita, a Hindu spiritual text.

6. **Wafers** Communion or Eucharist Wafers (bread).

ENTRY 36

1. **The Quantum Constructions** A cluster of holy buildings on the grounds of Rainbow Abbey used to recite the Divine Office of Trans-Benedictine Monastic Law.

2. **Orpheus** In Greek legend, the chief representation of the arts of song and the lyre, and of great importance in the religious history of Greece (Orphism).

3. **Kepler** Johannes Kepler (1571-1630). German mathematician, astronomer, astrologer, and key figure in the scientific revolution.

4. **Darwin** Charles Darwin (1809-1882). English naturalist who achieved lasting fame by producing considerable evidence that species originated through evolutionary change.

5. **Wittgenstein** Ludwig Wittgenstein (1889-1951). Austrian philospher of logic, language, and mind. Widely regarded as one of the most influential philosophers of the twentieth century.

6. **Vigils** A term for night prayer in Christianity.

7. The long poem is a critique of the negative aspects of post-modernism.

8. **Mahayana** See Entry 33, Note 4.

9. **Tendai** A Japanese school of Mahayana Buddhism.

10. **Soto** One of two major Japanese Zen sects (the other being Rinzai).

11. **Bhiku** A Buddhist mendicant monk.

12. **Koan** Zen Buddhist riddle used to focus the mind during meditation.

13. **Rinzai** One of two major Japanese Zen sects (the other being Soto).

14. **Zazen** See Entry 1, Note 13.

15. **Satori** Zen Buddhist term for enlightenment. Sometimes loosely used interchangeably with *Kensho*, the first perception of Buddha-Nature.

16. **Bardo** Period between death and rebirth when consciousness dwells in a bodiless condition and undergoes experiences determined by former meritorious and demeritorious actions.

ENTRY 37

1. **Original Testament** See Entry 16, Note 2.

2. **Brahman** See Entry 28, Note 7.

3. **Sufi** See Entry 1, Note 2.

4. **Shunyata** Emptiness. The nature of reality as it is understood in Mahayana Buddhism.

5. **Paradise Lost** Epic poem by seventeenth century English poet John Milton.

ENTRY 38

1. **Ophrys orchid** Also referred to as the "Bee orchids" due to the flowers of some species resemblance to the furry bodies of bumble bees or other insects.

2. **Dvorak** Antonin Dvorak (1841-1904). Czech composer of Romantic music.

3. **Catechism of the Catholic Church** See Entry 15, Note 3.

4. The information for this entry was found in Michael Pollan's *The Botany of Desire*.

ENTRY 39

1. **Allahu akbar** See Entry 1, Note 4.

2. **h-bar** In quantum mechanics it represents Dirac's constant, the reduced variant of Planck's constant.

3. **Planck's constant** A physical constant that is used to describe the sizes of quanta.

4. **Boson** In particle physics bosons are particles having integer spin.

ENTRY 40

1. **Kashmir** The northwestern region of the Indian subcontinent shared by India, Pakistan, and China. There have been frequent territorial disputes over Kashmir between India and Pakistan.

2. **Krishna** See Entry 1, Note 5.

3. **Triune** The triune brain.

4. **Sufi** See Entry 1, Note 2.

ENTRY 41

1. **Allah** See Entry 16, Note 7.

2. **Yule Tide Conifer** A Christmas tree.

3. **William James** American psychologist and philosopher (1842-1910). In his Gifford Lectures at the University of Edinburgh he provided a wide-ranging account of the varieties of religious experience.

4. **Berkeley** Irish philosopher George Berekely (1685-1753). Primarily known for his advancement of subjective idealism.

5. **Hume** Scottish philosopher David Hume (1711-1776) know for advocating a form of skepticism. Part one of this entry is about him and his ideas.

6. **Savages Noble** A term coined by philosopher Jean Jacques Rousseau (1712-1778).

7. **Kant** German philosopher Immanuel Kant (1724-1804). His *Critique of Pure Reason*, *Critique of Practical Reason*, and *Critique of Judgement* helped the modern age differentiate the good, the true, and the beautiful.

ENTRY 42

1. **Septuagint** See Entry 4, Note 4.

2. **Vulgate** See Entry 4, Note 3.

3. **Wycliffe** John Wycliffe (1320-1384). His English translation of the Bible is considered a precursor to the Protestant Reformation. He is called "The Morning Star of the Reformation."

4. **Tyndale** William Tyndale (1494-1536). Religious reformer and scholar who translated the Bible into the Early Modern English of his day.

5. **Coverdale** Miles Coverdale (1488-1568). Produced the first complete printed translation of the Bible into English.

6. **King James** See Entry 6, Note 7.

7. **Aramaic** Believed to have been the native language of Jesus.

8. **Gita** See Entry 35, Note 5.

9. For a better understanding of the sonnet research the Wilber-Combs lattice.

ENTRY 43

1. **First-tier consciousness** See Entry 6, Note 5.

2. **Napoleon** French emperor Napoleon Bonaparte (1769-1821).

3. **Don Quixote** Title character in the novel by Spanish auther Miguel de Cervantes.

4. **Baudelaire** French poet (1821-1867).

5. **Einstein** German theoretical physicist Albert Einstein (1879-1955).

6. **Dharma** See Entry 22, Note 2.

7. **Lila** See Entry 19, Note 2.

ENTRY 44

1. **Muld ad-Din ibn al-Arabi** See Entry 1, Note 7.

2. **Marcel Proust** French novelist (1871-1922).

3. **Gita** See Entry 35, Note 5.

4. **Samuel Beckett** Irish dramatist, novelist, and poet. See Entry 13, Note 1.

5. **Hajj** Pilgrimage to Mecca. One of the five pillars of the Islamic faith.

ENTRY 45

1. **Oporto** See Entry 34, Note 2.

2. **Prince Henry** See Entry 8, Note 2.

3. **Saint Ambrose** Roman Catholic saint (340-397).

4. **Compline** The last of seven separate canonical hours that are set aside for prayer each day in the Roman Catholic Church.

ENTRY 46

1. **Aleph-null** Used in a branch of mathematics called set theory. A set has cardinality aleph-null if and only if it is countably infinite.

2. **Cardinality** A measure of the number of elements in a set.

3. **Council of Constance** An ecumenical council of the Roman Catholic Church called in an attempt to end the papal schism which had resulted from the Avignon Papacy.

4. **Scutum fidei** Shield of the Trinity. A traditional Christian visual symbol representing the philosophy of the Holy Trinity.

5. **Martin V** His election ended the Western Schism. He was Pope from 1417 to 1431.

6. **Saint John of the Cross** See Entry 10, Note 4.

ENTRY 47

1. **Inferno** Part of *The Divine Comedy* written by Dante Alighieri between 1308 and 1321.

2. **Great Awakening** A period of dramatic religious revival in Anglo-American religious history.

3. **Shiva** See Entry 31, Note 7.

4. **Kaaba** A building inside of the great mosque in Mecca. It is the most holy site in the Islamic religion.

ENTRY 48

1. **Voltaire** French Enlightenment philosopher (1694-1778).

2. **Nietzsche** Prussian born philosopher Friedrich Nietzsche (1844-1900).

ENTRY 49

1. **Alfred North Whitehead** English mathematician and philosopher (1861-1947).

2. **Michel Foucault** French philosopher (1926-1984).

3. **Democritus** Pre-Socratic Greek philosopher.

4. **First-tier** See Entry 6, Note 5.

5. **World-centric** See Entry 1, Note 11.

ENTRY 50

1. **Vitruvian Man** The famous drawing by Leonardo da Vinci.

2. **Pardes** Term for the four levels of Jewish textual reading: Peshat (literal), Remez (allegorical), Derash (homiletically), and Sod (mystical). Translated into English it means orchard or paradise.

ENTRY 51

1. **Child Rabbinical Orchid in the Muslim Tao of Christ** Hugo Gustafson's nickname from Book One.

2. **Dominican** Popular name of the Roman Catholic Order of Preachers founded by Dominic of Osma in 1215. The Dominicans are a mendicant order, sharing with Franciscans a commitment to a life of poverty.

3. **Friars Minor** Another name for Franciscan.

4. **Theravadan Bhikku** A fully ordained male Buddhist monastic.

5. **Big-Top** A circus.

6. **The Slade** School of fine art in London.

7. **Ecole des Beaux-Arts** French for "school of fine arts". Refers to a number of influential art schools in France particularly in Paris.

8. **Sufi** See Entry 1, Note 2.

9. **Sikh Keshdhari Granthi** Keshdhari is a term which means "the long haired ones" which indicates a stricter observance of Sikh tenets. The granthi is the man or woman who performs reading of the Guru Granth Sahib at religious occasions.

10. **Guru Granth Sahib** Book of holy scripture for the Sikh faith. Granth is Punjabi for "book". Sahib is Hindi for "master".

ENTRY 52

1. **Yeshua** See Entry 7, Note 2.

2. **Gospel of Thomas** Modern name given to a New Testament-era apocryphon completely preserved in a papyrus Coptic manuscript discovered in 1945 at Nag Hammadi, Egypt.

3. **Nag Hammadi** Town in Egypt where, in 1945 thirteen leather-bound

papyrus codices were found by local peasants.

4. **Bodhisattva** A being who is dedicated to assisting all sentient beings in achieving complete Buddhahood. Literally means "enlightenment" in Sanskrit.

5. **Aggiornamento** Literally means "bringing up to date". It was one of the key words used during the Second Vatican Council.

6. For a better understanding of the "cross-hairs" mentioned in this entry, research Ken Wilber's "Four Quadrants" or "AQAL".

ENTRY 53

1. **St. Teresa of Avila** Carmelite nun and mystic (1515-1582).

2. **St. Peter's Square** Square located directly in front of St. Peter's Basilica in Vatican City.

3. **Vatican City** Papal enclave within the city of Rome.

ENTRY 54

1. This entry indicates the death of Pope Nicholas V.

2. **Isle of Man** Another name for Ambrojjio.

3. **Tao** See Entry 9, Note 5.

ENTRY 55

1. This entry was taken from Jack Miles *Christ: A Crisis in the Life of God*, pp. 44-45, Knopf, New York, 2001.

ENTRY 56

1. **Demiurge** In Gnostic and Platonic philosophies, the creator and controller of the material world.

2. **Tantric** Tantric yoga or tantrism refers to a collection of esoteric philosophes and spiritual practices found in several religions of Indian origin.

3. **Venus** Roman goddess of love.

4. **Apollo** Greek god of prophecy.

5. **Cosmic Microwave Background Radiation** A form of electromagnetic radiation discovered in 1965 that fills the entire universe.

6. **Isotropic** Having physical properties that do not vary with direction.

ENTRY 57

1. **The Five K's** Five articles of faith that some baptized Sikhs wear at all times.

2. Silas Paul's quote is from Sri Aurobindo's *The Life Divine*.

3. **Sri Aurobindo** Indian nationalist, scholar, poet, mystic, evolutionary phiolosopher, yogi and guru (1872-1950).

4. **Tat tvan asi** Sanskrit sentence meaning, "Thou art that."

ENTRY 58

1. **Natal Chart** The term used to describe a horoscope drawn for the exact time of an individual's birth at a particular place on Earth for the purposes of gaining information about the individual.

2. For a more elaborate explanation see Ken Wilber's "pre-trans fallacy".

ENTRY 59

1. **Stupa** Seen Entry 1, Note 12.

2. **Maimonides** Jewish rabbi, physician, and philosopher (1138-1204).

3. **Lotus Sutra** One of the most popular and influential Mahayana sutras and the basis on which the Tiantai and Nichiren schools of Buddhism were established.

4. **Duhkha** Sanskrit for "suffering". A central Buddhist concept (also spelled dukkha).

ENTRY 60

1. **Copernicus** Polish astronomer Nicolaus Copernicus (1473-1543).

2. **Heliocentric** Heliocentrism is the belief that the sun is the center of the Universe and or the Solar System.

ENTRY 61

1. **Mount Hira** A cave on the peak of Jabal al-Nour in the Hejaz region of present day Saudi Arabia. It is most notable for being the location where Muslims believe the prophet Muhammad received his first revelation from God.

2. **Ramadan** The fourth pillar of Islam and ninth month of the Islamic calendar.

3. **Gabriel** See Entry 25, Note 7.

4. **Recitation** See Entry 6, Note 6.

5. **Yeshua** See Entry 6, Note 2.

6. **Gethsemani** Garden where, according to the New Testament and Christian traditions, Jesus prayed the night before he was crucified.

7. **Ahmad ibn Majid** See Entry 20, Note 1.

8. **Hawiya** Arabic meaning a mother who has lost her first-born child underscored by a sense of falling into an abyss. See Entry 17 of Book One.

ENTRY 62

1. **Yeshua** See Entry 6, Note 2.

2. **Trans-Benedictine** See Entry 1, Note 3.

3. For a pointing exercise based on the various translations of the Qur'an see Entry 42 of Book One.

ENTRY 63

1. Quantum Catholic (or Integral Christian) holidays coupled with the corresponding astrological sign. Remember this is a pointing exercise and pay special attention to the surprise ending.

2. **Oblate** See Entry 28, Note 2.

ENTRY 65

1. **Persona** A social role or a character played by an actor. Basis for the English word "personality."

2. **Venus de Milo** Famous ancient Greek statue.

3. **Phantom limb** The sensation that an amputated or missing limb is still attached to the body.

4. **Taj Mahal** See Entry 2, Note 6.

ENTRY 66

1. **Rock flour** Particles of rock generated by glacial erosion. Also called glacial flour.

2. **Lila** See Entry 19, Note 2.

3. This entry was taken from Doug MacDougall's *Frozen Earth: The Once and Future Story of Ice Ages*.

ENTRY 67

1. **Cuius regio, eius religio** Latin for "Whose rule, his religion". In other words, the religion of the King or ruler would be the religion of the people.

2. **Monotheistic** A belief in the existence of one deity or God, or the oneness of God.

3. **Mandala** A generic term for any plan, chart or geometric pattern which represents the kosmos symbolically. A mandal, especially its center, can be used during meditation as an object for focusing attention.

4. **Ex divina pulchritudine esse omnium derivatur** Latin for "The being of all things is derived from the Divine Beauty".

ENTRY 68

1. **Triple Vision** See Entry 2, Note 8.

2. **Yeshua** See Entry 7, Note 2.

3. **Mount Olivet** Mountain ridge to the east of Jerusalem. Site of many important Biblical events.

4. **Nocturnal Journey** Journey made by the prophet Muhammad from Mecca to Jerusalem before ascending from the Masjid al-Aqsa to the heavens.

5. **Elijah** Prophet of the Hebrew Bible.

ENTRY 69

1. This entry is adapted from Eva de Vitray-Meyerovitch's *Rumi and Sufism*.

2. **Sama** Name for the ceremonies used by various Sufi orders which involve prayer, song, dance, and other ritualistic activities.

3. **Rumi** See Entry 1, Note 8.

4. **Itri** Turkish composer Buhurizade Itri (1640-1711).

5. **Ney** End blown flute that figures prominently in Middle Eastern music.

6. **Fire Sermon** Famous discourse of the Buddha.

7. **al-Ghalzali** Islamic theologian, philosopher, and mystic (1058-1111).

8. **Isra Miraj** Arabic terms for Muhammad's Night Journey and ascension. See Entry 68, Note 4.

9. **Sura** See Entry 6, Note 1.

ENTRY 70

1. **Prophet** See Entry 11, Note 4.

ENTRY 71

1. **Job** Character in the Book of Job in the Hebrew Bible. Also and Islamic prophet.

2. **Hasidic** A member of a Jewish movement of popular mysticism founded in Eastern Europe in the eighteenth century.

3. **Pope Benedict** See Entry 15, Note 2.

4. **Saint Peter** Christian saint and first Bishop of Rome.

5. **Atlas Shrugging** Allusion to *Atlas Shrugged*, a novel by Ayn Rand.

ENTRY 72

1. **Mantra** A religious syllable or poem, typically from the Sanskrit language.

2. **Trans-Benedictine** See Entry 1, Note 3.

3. **Noah** See Entry 8, Note 1.

ENTRY 73

1. An intertidal zone is an area of the foreshore and seabed that is exposed to the air at low tide and submerged at high tide.

ENTRY 74

1. **Thomas Aquinas** Saint Thomas Aquinas. Italian philosopher and theologian in the scholastic tradition (1225-1274). Considered by many to be the Catholic Church's greatest theologian.

2. **Augustine of Hippo** See Entry 33, Note 3.

3. **Yeshiva** Institution for Torah study.

4. **Monet** French painter Claude Monet (1840-1926).

5. **Tulku** A Tibetan Buddhist lama or other religious figure who has consciously decided to be reborn in order to continue his or her spiritual pursuits.

6. **Common, Special, Solitary, and Perfect** From *The Cloud of Unknowing*.

7. **Ex Oriente, lux!** Latin for: "From the East, Light!".

ENTRY 75

1. **Caldarium** Room with a hot plunge bath, used in a Roman bath complex.

2. **Saint Augustine** See Entry 33, Note 3.

ENTRY 76

1. **Bodhidharma** Buddhist monk traditionally credited as the founder of Chan (Zen) Buddhism in sixth century China.

ENTRY 77

1. **Nimbus** A bright halo or disk around the head of a deity, saint, or sovereign.

2. **Antinomian** Disagreeing with the philosophy that the same fixed rules and morality apply to everybody.

ENTRY 78

1. The poem is adapted from a poem by Ryokan.

ENTRY 79

1. **Prayer wheel** Tibetan Buddhist movable cylinder containing prayers.

2. **Red Guard** The Red Guards of China who aided in dismantling Tibet.

3. A play on Pope Benedict XVI's surname (Ratzinger).

4. **Saint Augustine** See Entry 33, Note 3.

5. **Shrove Tuesday** Term used to refer to the day before Ash Wednesday, the first day of Lent.

6. **Thomas Aquinas** See Entry 74, Note 1.

ENTRY 80

1. **Taj Mahal** See Entry 2, Note 6.

2. **Isra and mi'raj** See Entry 69, Note 8.

3. **Vedanta** See Entry 25, Note 9.

4. **Annamayakosa** The lowest of the five kosas or koshas. Kosas are the five cases or sheaths which cover the Atman in Hinduism.

5. **Fanaa** Sufi term for extinction. It means to annihilate the self while remaining physically alive.

6. **Prajna** Sanskrit for "wisdom". Prajna is the wisdom that is able to extinguish afflictions and bring about enlightenment.

7. **Guru Granth Sahib** See Entry 51, Note 10.

ENTRY 81

1. Information for this entry found in Charles Panati's *Sacred Origins of Profound Things*.

ENTRY 82

1. **Thomas Merton** Acclaimed Catholic theologian, poet, author, and social activist (1915-1968).

2. The quote in this entry was taken from Thomas Merton's *No Man is an Island*.

3. **First Noble Truth** Suffering or Dukkha.

ENTRY 84

1. **Heart Sutra** Well known Mahayana Buddhist sutra (Prajnaparamita class).

2. **Bodhisattva** See Entry 52, Note 4.

3. **Skandha** Five aggregates which categorize or constitute all individual experience according to Buddhist phenomenology.

ENTRY 85

1. **Sixth Manslon** A reference to Saint Teresa of Avila's *The Interior Castle*.

2. **Dark Night of the Soul** See Entry 10, Note 4.

ENTRY 86

1. **Lao Tze** Founder of Taoism and auther of the seminal Taoist work, the *Tao Te Ching*.

2. **Tao** See Entry 9, Note 5.

3. **Dharmakaya** The unmanifested aspect of a Buddha out of which Buddhas and indeed all phenomena arise and to which they return after their dissolution.

4. This entry was taken from Ken Wilber's *Up From Eden*, p. 251.

ENTRY 87

1. **Ganges** River in northern India considered holy by some Hindus.

ENTRY 89

1. The information for the first part of this entry was found in Neil De Grass Tyson and Donald Goldsmith's *Origins*.

2. **Erwin Schrodinger** Austrian physicist (1887-1961).

3. **Vedanta** See Entry 25, Note 9.

4. **Logos** The divine wisdom of the word of God.

ENTRY 90

1. **Ashoka** Emperor Ashoka the Great. Ruler of the Maurya Empire in present day eastern India from 273 BCE to 232 BCE and known for establishing monuments marking several significant sites in the life of Shakyamuni Buddha. According to Buddhist tradition he was closely involved in the preservation and transmission of Buddhism.

ENTRY 91

1. **Thermodynamics** The branch of physics that deals with conversions from one to another of various forms of energy and how these affect temperature, pressure, volume, mechanical action, and work.

2. **Agnosticism** The belief that it is impossible to know whether or not God exists.

ENTRY 92

1. **Ganesha** Hindu god that symbolizes intellect and wisdom. Usually depicted as a big-bellied, yellow or red god with four arms and the head of an elephant.

2. **Ramana Maharshi** Indian mystic (1879-1950).

3. **Dome of the Rock** Notable Islamic shrine/mosque in Jerusalem.

4. **Trilobite** Extinct arthropods in the class Trilobita.

5. **Constantinople** Capital of Roman Empire from330 to 395, the Byzantine Empire from 395 to 1453, and the Ottoman Empire from 1453 to 1923. Now called Istanbul.

ENTRY 93

1. **Mahamudra** Buddhist method of direct introduction to the nature of Mind (or Buddha-nature) and the practice of stabilizing the accompanying transcendental realization.

2. This entry was adapted from Tsele Natsok Rangdrol's *Lamp of Mahamudra*.

ENTRY 94

1. **Erasmus Grunewald** See Entry 34 in Book One.

2. **Samsara** See Entry 30, Note 4.

3. **Nirvana** Sanskrit word that means "extinction" or "extinguishing". This is not the transitory, sense-based happiness of everyday life, but rather an enduring transcendental happiness integral to the calmness attained through enlightenment.

ENTRY 97

1. **Templars** See Entry 25, Note 6.

ENTRY 98

1. **Chandogya Upanishad** One of the principle Upanishads commented upon by Adi Shankara.

2. **Brahman** See Entry 28, Note 7.

ENTRY 99

1. **Dogen** Founder of the Soto school of Zen Buddhism (1200-1253).

2. **Vesak** Holiday celebrated as the Buddha's birthday.

(WHY I'M) NO LONGER STARVING FOR AN ADEQUATE MYTH

MICHAEL GARFIELD

I am the voice of a generation starving for an adequate myth. Myths are the carriers and conduits of a vision - the metaphors and narratives around which we organize and accrete our understanding. Every generation has come together within a mythology, and used it to push forward into its fruition. In a way, we are nourished by our myths in return for fulfilling them.

It must be said that my generation has more mythology from which to choose than any before it. We stand before a global buffet of stories, food of all flavors, information crashing in from all sides, an unprecedented panoply of cultural richness. What we lack is an organizing directive, some way to *handle* all of this humanity without shrinking from its light or dissolving into incoherence at the spectacular diversity of it all. Imagine everyone in the cafe trying to force-feed you simultaneously, and you'll get the idea. In spite of our wealth of culture, we hunger for genuine, hopeful, reconstructive narratives – that is, *integral* myths. Almost no one is telling my generation, or those to come, what to do with this orgiastic diversity of experience. Our myth has been one of dissipation, of dissolution – the end of oil, the end of modernity, the end of the biosphere, the end of western hegemony, the end of science, the end of childhood. We are born into a world that has come together just in time to discover it is breaking apart.

But Paul Lonely is changing all of that. What Paul is doing for us - the generation growing up alongside the academic reconstruction of integral theory - is offering us a new mode of experiencing these truths. And, I would like to note, Paul is a name with quite a pedigree for getting the word out.

Freed from the conventional trappings of historical spiritual texts, blindingly aware of its own cultural embeddedness and laughing at it compassionately, Suicide Dictionary belongs in a thin pantheon with the paintings of Alex Grey as a message for and from our collective future. It is playful and colorful and fluid, in stark opposition to even the most inspiring theories of the world into which we walk with one eye open. That Paul has used language to communicate this utterly translinguistic vision is a testament to his cleverness – his book is winking at all of us from behind the veil, like the Tao Te Ching or its formal predecessor, the Upanishads. Every page rings brightly with the cause to which he is devoted.

Occasionally he explicates this, lamenting how the transformational power of one religion's symbols are woefully unavailable to those of other faiths. This power "sits trapped in their brains like a living fossil," buried under the ancient strata of consciousness, waiting to be excavated, integrated, and activated. The injunction? To "encourage a generation of spiritual archeologists." The gears of faith have ground to a halt, and it is time to cultivate a catalytic movement, a generation whose "vocation is the transference of energy to the intermeshing gear in waiting."

With that, we embark on a voyage of impossible fullness, through the world's vast traditions of spirituality and natural science. The illustrative endnotes alone are worth the price of this book; many of these terms are indeed "living fossils" for practitioners of traditions unfamiliar with them; he's doing us a service by bringing them together in one volume (not to mention articulating them in such a lucid way). Suddenly we have a codex.

Paul has a gift for taking the omnicultural perspective and effortlessly weaving it into his dialogue, like these are ordinary things for people to say: "If Saladin had four arms in a Polaroid, what would he hold in the palm of each hand?" Islam, Hindu, and Technology are all partying in the same casual thought experiment. These are the conversations that felt scandalous even in a 21st Century liberal arts college. But while I'm skinny dipping, Paul's Quantum Catholics are taking a bath.

Of course, they're also occasionally *streaking* through the Garden(s), nicknaming their surrogate son things like Child Rabbinical Orchid of the Muslim Tao of Christ – a title that my inner Paleontologist tried to piece together for a minute before handing over the reigns to the Master.

Suicide Dictionary is spilling over with this kind of contemporary koan, just like how the boughs of the monastery grounds swell heavy with fruit of all persuasions. Practicing ludicrous abundance, the monks dance in and out of every room, always popping in at opportune moments to offer some gloriously relevant irreverence (when electrons do this, quantum physicists call it "tunneling" – as in, spelunking – as in, the first temple was a cave).

Play as the highest realization – skywriting, throwing stones or floating them on leaves, plunging into endless word games and sculpture and "tasmanianly swiveling" in swiveling chairs. This is the world when nobody is laying claim to all of the truth. There is *so* much to go around, far more than any of us could ever use up, and the Quantum Catholics find it just as easily expounding gleefully on back-propagation through neural networks as they do in the contemplation of their officially holy scripts. I've never encountered such a sublime sense of humor, one so embedded in existential language. He writes of his characters standing at the edge of a room:

"Existing in the boundaries of Silas Paul's studio"

He describes the slow circuit of the day:

"As Sunday afternoon wriggles its way into the imaginations of the northern hemispheres"

Paul infuses his prose and characters alike with this conspiratorial glee. Play is like sand for them! It gets into everything – between the fibers of one's clothing, into one's hair; it's just as *there* when one steps out of the shower, and it is *certainly* there in the cloisters and baths, and in every compassionate word we catch as it passes from one Quantum to another.

They are leading my generation by example – we, the children of information, who are inexorably being drawn to repudiate the laissez-faire world in which we have fledged and to dream together cities in which the world is ever felt; where the first rule of economy is the giving of gifts; where there's something familiar about everyone (even "strangers"); where we are careful with the size of our footprint but adventurous with the length of our stride.

I am of a generation that plays to forget the world we have inherited, somehow both painfully aware of our heavy next hundred years and steeped black in denial. It is an amazing thing to have this book that says, "You have all that you need to laugh, to express something inexhaustible and infinitely powerful in its priority. You can move into the world from this home beyond place, clothed in bliss, breathing a wakeful smile onto the troubled brows of your brothers and sisters." How else can we expect to meet our times where they challenge us, if not in exuberance and wizened fearlessness, in loving lightness?

Paul isn't wont to lecture us on the intricate meta-philosophy that is guiding his hand; other people, our specialists in generalization, are already doing that work. Nonetheless, he does sow hints throughout, glancing us past the monks' celebratory academics, in which (it seems) everyone is already informed. The recitation of theology or science or literature is more incantation than education. We are less learning than remembering. Even when one of Paul's liminal characters is getting corrected, at great length and with the full boisterous thrush of declaration, it doesn't feel like a lecture.

These are pointing instructions dressed up as a college education – *if only* more so-called liberal arts institutions were living up to their name and providing us with such grand scope and synthesis! The science breathes naturally in this text, secure, unafraid that it will have to spend its all fighting to assert itself against the night. Evolutionary biology and other modern esoteric sports have finally been invited to the dinner table with the Septuagint. (After all, doesn't the Dalai Lama love listening to neurobiologists?) The transcendental It, the body of the world, is the described and investigated Divine – the third in the room with two lovers. Take whatever the world gives you and worship it, Paul tells us over and over and over. This is my body. This is my blood (and it's ABO – even the *blood* is integral!).

Voices are liberated by acknowledgment, and Paul liberates science into the service of its eternal lover, Mystery. Sneezing from allergies, one of his monks shrugs: "You know my tendency to pollinate myself." (That's a monk taboo joke *and* an evolution joke!) In one passage, the monks speak of Yeshua as "heterozygous for every trait," and then bounce into a foxy little debriefing on Mendelian genetics as a metaphor of Christian mysticism. In another, random acts of human kindness are affirmed by introspection as instances of natural selection (some might call it Grace). Nature, red in tooth and claw, is delivered with a pirouette ("Frogs and crickets are competing to out-scream one another."). Not since Annie Dillard shared her poetic hermitage in the 70's have the burning bush and the invisible river received such a tender paean. Yeah, evolution loves death, God is an amnesiac mad scientist – but why so glum? Seen through Paul's rose windows, green's infatuation with black had me tickled pink.

At Rainbow Abbey, every fact and interpretation is cherished. In the same breath that he twists the canon with a bit of historical accuracy and replaces Eve's impossible apple with the more likely pomegranate (native to the fertile crescent), he pulls us beyond such specificities and the Fall, proclaiming that, "Divine was the Apple that forced me to pray." Indeed. Thank you, salvific pome, anonymous and prehistoric bearer of seeds, whatever you "actually" were.

Everything gets duly recognized for its divinity, here. Pollinating again, Paul gives Eve's pomegranate an origin to compete with Christ's own Immaculate Conception:

"Two flowers not random this Powder adhered,
An insect of God was transported by wind,
It landed on Carpels that Silence had cleared
For Seeds of Example our Farmers will tend."

Silence has cleared the flower's carpels, and the pollinating insect is God's. The flowers are not random. Are we still talking about evolution? Yes! Paul's story of the world is humming beyond the highest limits of hearing, stretching us up into silent attention. His writing takes the mundane and accelerates it to the speed of light, centrifuging superficialities to the periphery and leaving bare the spinning center of it all.

And does it spin! Everywhere I look, Suicide Dictionary is an enzo: The Circle of Gardens, swiveling chairs, boomeranging rocks, celestial spheres, buzzing subatomic strings, circadian rhythms and annual metaphors, talk of swallowing the moon, the inward arc, the sweeping grace of a skywriter, the "Discoid flowers of tansy," playing symbiosis with a disc in the sky, the unlubricated Ferris wheel of mythic religion…and on and on. Paul's lilies may not toil, but they *do* spin, free from the gravity of our desperate attempts to make sense of life before we live it.

In another departure from the myths of prior eras, Suicide Dictionary is written almost entirely in present tense – all the better for shaking the dust of narrative thinking off of one's prose-encoded pointing instructions. The point isn't so much to tell us how we got here and what we are meant to do (although these are not left unexplored), but to remind us that we *are*, at all. With its gaze turned towards the eternal timeless now of enlightened awareness, most of this book can't be bothered with a linear temporal sequence. Instead, it relies on an assemblage of moments we can only assume are happening more or less in order. But why bother with such an assumption? This is the helical time of the abbey, not the secular calendar of the city. When historical narrative *does* appear, it's again in service of fecundity – the diaspora of Islam, sewn into the origin myth of the banana (a cultigen that, for all it provides us, relies on our care to persist). Fruit as history, and history as fruit. The world as an endless play of impossible bounty.

What husbandry! Floral fantasies, playfully elusive syntax, and characters we discover through their voices and not abstract top-down generalizations: this is what Burroughs might have written if he'd found Big Mind instead of heroin.

I learned a lot reading this book – and more still on the second pass, because its subtleties aren't all to be gotten at once. Paul doesn't offer his truths in the digestible condescension so common to contemporary art. His prose is vibrant with the same exotic matter-of-factness that permeates his poetry. If, as some of my friends have said, learning integral is like learning a whole new language, then Suicide Dictionary is an immersion course, dropping us without warning or excuse into a world we slowly and naturally internalize. It is an injunction: the desire to reap a fuller knowing from this text had me consulting my own "normal" dictionary with…well, a religious fervor. In all of its support, its incredible loving inclusiveness, this book doesn't kid about the challenge it presents us, which is no less that the complete recasting of our own language and being in the light of something far more lush, fluid, and creative than even poets are willing to admit. It forced me to look things up! It evoked in me the same eager monastic scholarship so gleefully flaunted by its floret of a nonet.

Paul is proof that creativity will attach itself to anything and push its roots out, flowering. Take for example this book, blooming from the dry sand of Merriam Webster's – and just the first hundred entries, no less! It's quite a body to weave from *air*, and a tremendous homage to the tradition of all flora (and thus all fauna). This is a reconstruction par excellence, living proof that one of the least poetic texts in the language can still be fertile soil for the wave of reclamation – that the bones of thought do not sit in a museum but scaffold an endless, pliant quickening. Paul has spread a mural of sacred graffiti on the concrete wall of our skyscraping industrial lexicon, and much like his brothers in paint, he has issued a powerful reminder that *this is our space.* Language is *our* garden and we can grow in it what we please.

This is a message light years beyond the reliance on expert interpretation, beyond coming to our own conclusions, beyond even the pluralist mystique of everyone's own secret tongue. This is a call to arms – if arms are boughs, and offer rather than take. It is a manifesto for future (and present) generations who are coming awake to the strength of the illuminated word. Suicide Dictionary says: you look it up; you tell me what I mean; let us stand together in the infinite mystery of the mundane, swallow the moon – and, while we're at it, let's cover it in tattoos. Nobody familiar with this book can ever tease me again about reading the dictionary. (Next stop: the phone book.)

As if he were writing about his own text (and not just about the human brain stem), Paul incants,

"Better use it...to create a group of philosopher kings. First, teach them what we teach. Infest the world with an integral awareness of higher embrace and an un-ending curiosity for book-learning and the depths of contemplation. Then, teach them a working knowledge of biomolecular and quantum computational technologies. A sub-class of men, such as these, are already rising."

And there it is. *This* is the significance of Suicide Dictionary to my generation.

So. Paul *Lonely* – both personal and anonymous. Ken Wilber is apparently fond of telling Paul that his readers haven't been born yet. (Henry Miller says loneliness is a prerequisite for great art - how appropriate.) I have to disagree with Ken – breathlessly, having to stop in awe after nearly every passage, I read Suicide Dictionary, and I loved it.

Then again, maybe I haven't been born yet.

Either way, Paul won't be Lonely for long. In a brilliantly integral pass, he is asking all of us to help realize the rest of this ongoing creation that is Suicide Dictionary. His call to integral artists is about to blow open an incredible new movement of trans-formative creativity (for which the art world is starving, after half a century of translation), a multimedia orgasm of the gift and receipt of sacred art. There are as many dimensions of free interpretation as there are artists. Monks have always loved devotional illustration; perhaps we'll see The Illuminated Suicide Dictionary, with each poem rendered in luminous calligraphy and paint? Music has always held the soul and its poetry in the same embrace; my soul stirs to imagine The Liturgy of the Quantum Heart, with sacred dance and musical performance. Lord only knows how people might translate something like this to film, but given the readership I imagine it's only a matter of time before we have Suicide Dictionary in a webcast serial or as the pet project of the Integral

Actors Studio (where we're breaking down not just the fourth wall, but also the fifth, and sixth).

We've only begun. Welcome aboard. This book is the first step in something truly beautiful, and good, and true. And as for Paul himself: I think I speak for my generation when I say,

Respecting the partial nature
Of this truth and
Care, We as the
Kosmos
Salute him.

Michael Garfield
Lawrence, Kansas
April, 2007